authentic cambodian recipes

from mother to daughter

authentic cambodian recipes

from mother to daughter

Sorey Long with Kanika Linden

Editor: Lydia Leong
Designer: Bernard Go Kwang Meng
Photographers: Kanika Linden and Jérome Jaymond (pages 12, 26, 27 and 232)

Original title: Au pays de la Pomme Cythère
Original edition © 2009 White Tara Ltd

English translation © 2010 White Tara Ltd
Design © 2010 Marshall Cavendish International (Asia) Pte Ltd
Reprinted 2013

Published by Marshall Cavendish Cuisine
An imprint of Marshall Cavendish International

Other Marshall Cavendish Offices:

Marshall Cavendish Corporation. 99 White Plains Road, Tarrytown NY 10591-9001, USA • Marshall Cavendish International (Thailand) Co Ltd. 253 Asoke, 12th Flr, Sukhumvit 21 Road, Klongtoey Nua, Wattana, Bangkok 10110, Thailand • Marshall Cavendish (Malaysia) Sdn Bhd, Times Subang, Lot 46, Subang Hi-Tech Industrial Park, Batu Tiga, 40000 Shah Alam, Selangor Darul Ehsan, Malaysia.

National Library Board, Singapore Cataloguing-in-Publication Data

Long, Sorey,¬ 1941-
Authentic Cambodian recipes : from mother to daughter /¬ Sorey Long & Kanika Linden. – Singapore : Marshall Cavendish Cuisine, c2010.
p. cm.
Includes bibliographical references and index.
ISBN-13 : 978-981-4276-86-3

1. Cooking, Cambodian. 2. Cookbooks. I. Linden, Kanika.
II. Title.

TX724.5
641.59596 -- dc22 OCN644920340

Printed in Malaysia by Times Offset (M) Sdn Bhd

Contents

Dedication

To the memory of Ouk Bou, my beloved mother, to my daughters Lida and Kanika and my granddaughter Séléna, and to all the women who are passionate about food.

Sorey Long

To the beautiful Khmer women, custodians of Cambodian culinary traditions.

Kanika Linden

Foreword

This book was born out of love. The love of food, of sharing, and of spending time together as mother and daughter. In many ways, the latter was the strongest motivation for this project. Laughing, crying, hugging, waiting, sulking, giggling, Kanika and Sorey have done it all during the four years it took to write this book. How else could it be, really? Can you imagine having to record your mother's thoughts and recipes on paper? It is no mean feat in itself, but it turns into even more of a challenge when your mother lives a few thousands kilometres away and can practically cook with her eyes shut.

"So, mum, how much palm sugar do you need for this recipe?"

"Well, you know, not too much, you kind of get a sense of it. You start with a bit and if it is not enough, you add a little more until it tastes right."

"Hmm, right... okay then... so, would you say... about a spoonful?"

"A spoonful? Oh, I see... let me think... what do you mean? A teaspoon?"

"Hmm, I guess... "

"Wait... hmm, no, good heavens no, that's way too much. About a coffee spoon at the most, you need to be very precise you know, otherwise you'll confuse people!"

"Right... "

And so the conversation continued, between the highly trained, experienced and intuitive chef and her patient, determined, methodical daughter. The synergies grew as time went by, and having had the privilege of witnessing working sessions in their London kitchen, I can confirm that this book grew out of love and in turn allowed love to grow to another level between these two exceptional women.

Kanika says she has finally got to know her mother and that most of the book has been one long chat. The introduction for instance, started as a series of questions, with Kanika finding out about her mother's life, about what it was like to be a child in Cambodia in the 1940s. As her life unfolded, Kanika learnt about her family and the budding of her mother's passion for food. She learnt about herself, her older sister Lida, her grandparents, their marriage, and about life a century ago. For both of them, and many others in the family, this was a journey of reconnection.

Reading the introduction, I realised how Cambodians talk about themselves in an understated way. What would otherwise be considered an achievement, an extraordinary resilience against the odds (war, hunger, loss), just gets mentioned in passing. Modesty, gratitude, generosity and a constant sense of wonder, exude from this family. Seeing their astonished faces when they were handed the Gourmand

World Cookbook Awards trophy for the "Best Asian Cuisine Cookbook in the World" in Paris was a pure treat. "What? We won? Really? Oh, wow… Really?..." Their speech was unprepared, but like this book, it was authentic and came from the heart.

The momentum this book has generated is quite remarkable.

The book has brought families closer together. Uncles, brothers, sisters, cousins and long lost friends have come to offer help, skills and time. Some of the wounds of separation and exile are starting to heal. Family and friends have rediscovered Cambodian cuisine, their home country and their own identity. Most importantly, the book has given Sorey a sense of pride and achievement.

It has changed perceptions, of women and traditions, of heritage and pride, of limits and possibilities. It has inspired others to be creative and brought hidden talents to the fore— Sorey the fascinating storyteller and Kanika, the self-taught food photographer.

Writing this book required perseverance, trust, creativity and openness. It was hard work and both Sorey and Kanika worked with all their heart on this project. The trips back and forth to Cambodia, the countless recipes cooked and tested, the dishes styled, the hundreds of photos taken and redone twice to reach the right standards, the exacting formatting and proofreading have been worth it.

This book, born out of love, has been an adventure, a journey of reconnection. Cambodia's recent history is one of war, violence and suffering. In this book, Sorey and Kanika chose to present a different facet of Cambodia, one which is beautiful and nurturing: Khmer culinary traditions.

Valérie Rosenberg-Weston

Introduction

Culinary experiences have always been woven into my life. Scents and flavours of food trigger memories, stories and long forgotten emotions which come tumbling back from the past.

An Improbable Union: Srok Sre and Srok Chamcar

I was born in 1941 in the village of Rocakandal in the Cambodian province of Kratie. My father, Pol Soeung[1] and my mother Ouk Bou, named me Sorey.

My father was from a village called Preah Ream in the Takeo province, a deprived region where soils are mostly infertile. Cambodians refer to this type of region as the land of the rice fields (*srok sre*). Indeed, except for sugar palm trees (*tnoat*), only rice for subsistence is produced there.

My father was highly educated, thanks to the determination of his own father, Pol Tith. A respected and well-read village chief, Pol Tith sent his son to study among Buddhist monks, and then to Phnom Penh, the capital, as no primary school was available locally. Upon finishing his studies, my father became a civil servant, starting as assistant to the clerk of the court. He was a hardworking man and got promoted quickly. He became head of district (*chauvay srok*[2]) in the Kratie province and then governor (*chauvay khet*[2]) of Stung Treng, a northern province of Cambodia.

With my parents and siblings in front of our family home, Stung Treng, 1948. I was 7 years old (pictured extreme right).

My mother, on the other hand, was born in the village of Taluon, in the Kandal province. Her village was located on the banks of the Mekong River where vegetation is lush and crops abundant. Cambodians call this fertile region the land of the gardens and fields (*srok chamcar*). Along with rice and tobacco, the rich soil allows the cultivation of a wide array of fruit and vegetables such as white radishes, corn, beans, cucumbers, bananas, sapodillas[3], coconuts and kapok[4].

My mother came from the largest family in Taluon. Even today, most of the villagers there are direct descendants of my great-grandfather, Ta Prak. My mother's family was prosperous and owned several plots of land. Most of what they produced was bartered for rice and palm sugar with villagers from the *srok sre*.

Ouk Bou was the eldest of six children, one boy and five girls. As such, very early on in life, she had to take up work normally reserved for men. Ploughing, harvesting and working in the fields had taken priority over education for her. Although she could hold a man's place behind the plough, my mother had little notion of cooking, sewing, reading or writing.

The marriage of my parents looked, on the surface, rather improbable: an educated man and an illiterate woman who barely knew how to be a good housewife. The truth is that their marriage was one of convenience. It cemented the strong relationships developed through trade between the villagers of the *srok chamcar* and the *srok sre*.

Delicacies from the Provinces: Grilled Crickets and Red Ants

Early in his career while head of a district, my father travelled often throughout the province. As a mark of their gratitude, villagers welcomed him with delicacies. I recall particularly exciting ones such as snake soup, tortoise served with fermented fish sauce (*prahok*), fried crickets, silkworms, red ants and bee larvae. These were all prepared, cooked and eaten in a very special way.

Crickets (*chan reth*), a good source of protein, were either grilled and salted or simply deep-fried. If they happened to contain eggs, their heads and legs would be chopped off and a peanut would be stuffed inside just before cooking, as an added treat.

Silkworms (*doek doeur*), a by-product of silk extraction, were another delicacy. After boiling the cocoons to unravel the silk thread, the silkworms were collected and served as an appetiser or as a main course with rice. They were sometimes also grilled and served as a delicious accompaniment to noodle dishes such as rice vermicelli with green sauce (*nom ban chok samlar khmer*).

Red ants (*ang krang*) were tricky to prepare as the villagers had to collect them from trees and avoid being bitten in the process. This involved shaking the trees until the ant nests fell into buckets of salted water. The ants would float to the surface of

the water while the eggs sank to the bottom. They were left in the water for a whole day before being served with grilled fish (*trey aing*). This delicacy was often offered to Buddhist monks during the Cambodian New Year (Chaul Chnam) festivities.

As a child, my favourite treat was grilled bee larvae flavoured with a pinch of salt. I loved their crunchy texture and incredible taste which oscillated between honey and salt. This snack is still very popular today as I found out during a recent visit to the Rattanakiri province.

My Childhood: Buttered Baguettes and Nom Kang

My mother started her married life with no cooking experience. Learning to cook became an urgent necessity. She spent the first few weeks of her marriage spying on her neighbour through the gaps in the palm leaf walls of her house. This was how she learnt the popular dishes of her native Kandal region.

When my father was promoted to become governor of Stung Treng, my parents moved into the governor's mansion, an imposing colonial-style house. As the governor's wife, my mother was expected to entertain. Receptions became a regular event, and my mother, aided by her newly appointed chef and several helpers, prepared elaborate meals with great attention to detail. Menus became increasingly sophisticated and dishes such as curries and *mi bam pong*[5] started appearing on our dining table.

The food that we ate every day at home was plentiful and varied, with a mix of Cambodian and French cuisine. I have fond memories of those days, with buttered baguettes in the morning, soups, fried fish and stir-fries (*t'cha*) for lunch and dinner, and amazing afternoon teas. Those afternoon teas still make my mouth water as I recall the French patisseries (*nom baraing*) served alongside traditional Cambodian delicacies such as caramelised sticky rice cakes (*nom kang*) and charcoal-grilled sticky rice and banana rolls (*nom an sam chek aing*), page 174.

The Years of Hardship: Nom Kriep and Pha'ak Chienn

During his tenure as governor of the Stung Streng province, my father fell ill and died a year later at the age of 41. That was 1949 and I was eight years old. Now a widow with four children and without any resources to make a living, my mother had to leave the family home and move to Phnom Penh to stay with relatives. These were tough times for her, but my mother's incredible resilience and resourcefulness helped her manage the transition and she did her best to shelter us from hardship.

She took on a myriad of menial jobs to feed us. From sewing to selling wood and cakes, she somehow managed to provide for us.

Selling cakes at the market was a tiring and difficult job that generated little income. My mother and older sister Sarabory would wake up before sunrise, light a fire and prepare thin, crispy pancakes (*nom kriep*). To make these pancakes, my mother would grind glutinous rice and rice, add palm sugar and fat to the mixture, form round pancakes, sun-dry, then fry them. They would also prepare cakes made with several coloured layers of rice, coconut milk and sugar (*chak chan*) as well as sticky rice balls filled with palm sugar (*nom plè aye*), page 163. I would sell the cakes after school and for all this work, we would only earn one riel (about three cents[6]) for two pancakes.

Early in the morning before going to school, breakfast for me would be rice soup (*babar*) with fried fermented fish (*pha'ak chienn*). My mother would stir-fry garlic, shallots and ginger strips in a wok greased with lard. With the rest of the fat, she would fry the fermented fish and caramelise it with palm sugar. For lunch and dinner, we would have a simple sour soup with water spinach (*samlar m'chou trakuon*) or grilled fish (*trey aing*) served with rice. At teatime, I had rice flour pancakes (*nom am bèng*), seasoned with salt and fresh aromatic herbs (*t'chi*).

When my father was alive, dishes were elaborate and abundant. After his death, our meals were simple and frugal, consisting mainly of rice, fish, *pha'ak* and inexpensive vegetables. Somehow, my memories of these simple dishes are more vivid. Poverty creates hunger and this makes flavours more pronounced.

Leaving the Nest: University Canteen and Saramann

By the time my turn came to leave the nest, our financial situation had improved. My older sister got married at 18[7] and my brother had found a good job. He encouraged me to further my studies and I joined the Tonle Bati training centre to become an adult education teacher[8]. I topped my class and was offered a job as a teacher at the centre. In 1966, I obtained a six-month grant from UNESCO to study adult education in France.

I met Long Botta, my husband-to-be in Toulouse in the south of France. He also had a bursary and had been studying science for seven years at Paul Sabatier University in Toulouse. With his meagre grant, he could not afford a trip home to Cambodia. When I met him, he was homesick and missing Cambodian food. In those days, no restaurant in France offered anything resembling Cambodian cuisine, and even if there had been one, he would not have been able to afford it. Very few shops stocked Asian food, and even if they had, he had no idea how to cook. As a result, he took all his meals at the university canteen, which fed him but did not fulfill his longing for home cooking.

I was also living on the campus and decided one day to organise a Khmer dinner party for all the Cambodian students. My mother had sent me a little parcel from Cambodia containing *saramann* paste[9], a key ingredient of Khmer cuisine. Without it, I would not have been able to cook Cambodian curry! While getting things ready in the kitchen that day, I suddenly realised I had forgotten the condiment in my dormitory. I sent a friend upstairs to fetch it. On his way, he bumped into Long Botta in the corridor and invited him to the party. That brief encounter sealed our destiny. Long Botta was a bit nervous as he didn't have much to wear and didn't have a present, but he came to the party in a borrowed suit and with a lovely rose that he had picked up in a public garden. I still don't know whether it was me or my *saramann* that captured his heart, but he fell in love with me that night.

Motherhood: Green Mangoes, Duck Egg Delicacy and Camembert Cheese

After we returned to Cambodia in 1967, Long Botta began courting me. He sent me hundreds of roses and worked hard to be in my brother's good graces. As the eldest man of the family, my brother's approval was essential to my marriage agreement, so Long Botta invited him regularly to dine at restaurants. Almost every cent of his modest teacher's salary was spent on getting us to like him. Won over by his patience and persistence, my family eventually agreed to the wedding. We married in 1968. Shortly after, I became pregnant with my first daughter, Lida.

Whoever said that pregnant women crave strawberries? For my eldest daughter Lida, I had no particular food craving but my husband became obsessed with eating up to 10 green *svay l'hong*[10] mangoes a day, seasoned with crushed coarse salt and chillies.

When pregnant with my second daughter Kanika, I started craving half-hatched duck eggs (*pong tear konn*). These are partly incubated duck eggs with half-formed chicks inside. Connoisseurs check on the age of the chicks when buying the eggs from market sellers, as the younger the chick, the softer the bones and the more succulent the egg. Boiled for about 15 minutes, they are eaten in the shell and are typically seasoned with salt, pepper, a dash of lemon juice and plenty of fresh aromatic herbs (*t'chi*).

I would eat one a day but there was once when I ended up gobbling 30! From that day on, the mere mention of half-hatched duck eggs became unbearable and I had to cover my ears when street hawkers walked past crying out their interminable litanies:

Pong tear konn (Duck eggs)
Pong tear konn (Duck eggs)
Pong tear kâr mean konn (Duck eggs with chicks)
Konn kâr mean pong tear (Chicks with duck eggs)

While this was clearly an unusual craving, I also remember fantasising about cheese, a very rare delicacy in Cambodia in those days[11]. One evening in 1970, I suddenly craved for cheese, but the night curfew prevented me from going out[12]. Mild to start with, the craving gradually intensified and I was crying my eyes out as it had become unbearable. By midnight, my husband took pity on me. He knocked on the door of our French neighbours, Monique and Christian Desremeaux and begged for some cheese. To this day, I have never tasted a better piece of Camembert.

Embassy Receptions and Dinner Parties: Golden Angel Hair and Nataing

With a nuclear physics PhD in hand, my husband started his career in 1967 as a professor in Physics and Chemistry at the Faculty of Sciences of Phnom Penh Royal University. He was quickly promoted to senior government positions[13] and became Minister of Culture in 1975, aged 33. As his wife, I was expected to entertain, organise galas and receptions for foreign ambassadors and members of government, just as my mother was.

I became a member of the International Women's Association, a club that brought together women of different nationalities. We hosted tea parties and organised cooking lessons where I learned to prepare many French, Australian and American dishes. At the Japanese embassy, I discovered the art of floral composition, ikebana. At receptions, I picked up many ideas on food presentation and table decoration. Combined with my own family traditions of carving fruit and vegetables into beautiful ornamental objects[14], my receptions and cooking became increasingly refined and creative. Dishes such as golden angel hair, a dessert made with egg yolks and sugar, crispy rice cakes with *nataing* sauce (*nataing*), page 148, and fish *amok* (*amok trey*), page 74, appeared on our menus.

Leaving Cambodia and Settling in France: Ham and Chicory Gratin with Béchamel Sauce

Following the fall of Phnom Penh in 1975, we left Cambodia for the United States, then settled in France in 1977. These were tough times. Uprooted, we had lost everything, our country, our family and our hope. We felt isolated, cut off from our compatriots and struggled to adapt to the new language, food and cold weather. My husband found a job as a medical physicist in Chaumont in the Haute-Marne department and I was due to start work at a sewing factory.

One day my neighbour, Michèle Hemery invited me for lunch. She was making baked chicories wrapped in ham and served with béchamel sauce (*gratin d'endives au jambon*). As she taught me how to make béchamel sauce[15], we chatted about our lives and backgrounds and shared our culinary experiences. She suggested I give up my job at the sewing factory and contact her brother. He was headmaster in a secondary school and was looking to recruit a teacher. I applied for the position and was appointed teacher[16] of vocational training and home economics. From then, I had a soft spot for ham and chicory gratin as this simple dish with its béchamel sauce started a long lasting friendship with my neighbour and was the beginning of a new life for me in France.

Learning French Cooking: Genoese Sponge and Samlar M'chou Sour Soup

As part of my job, I realised that I had to acquire the basics of French cuisine very quickly. I dived into cookbooks and did work placements to gain both theoretical and practical knowledge. There was an occasion when I was working for several weeks in a bakery. There, I learnt the art of making *viennoiseries*[17], *genoese* sponge, puff pastry and shortbread dough, and also discovered the importance of food preservation and hygiene, nutrition and new cooking methods.

These new skills strongly influenced my cooking and even changed the way I prepared Cambodian dishes. For instance, the traditional way of preparing the classic *samlar m'chou* sour soup was to boil the fish first, followed by the vegetables. This generally resulted in overcooked, dried and crumbly fish. I applied my new knowledge to these old recipes and boiled the vegetables first, adding the fish at the very end for a few minutes only.

Embracing French Culture: Five-spice Stuffed Duck and Coq Au Vin

As the years passed, our food habits and home cooking were gradually enriched and influenced by French cuisine. Dishes such as *poule au pot* (chicken stew) and *coq au vin* (chicken cooked in red wine) started appearing on our dining table alongside traditional Cambodian stir-fries (*t'cha*), soups (*samlar*), Khmer steamboats (*tch'hav han khmer*), page 108, and five-spice stuffed duck (*tear tim*), page 95. I introduced my family to such French culinary traditions as the *galette des rois* (a rich almond cake eaten on the twelfth night after Christmas), foie gras (a duck liver delicacy), frog legs and even escargots cooked in garlic butter. France is also renowned for its regional specialties, and my husband and children thoroughly approved of *choucroute* (a sauerkraut-based dish with sausages and pork) and *bouillabaisse* (a typical rich fish soup from southern France), if not the *lapin à la moutarde* (rabbit in mustard sauce).

Reconnecting with Compatriots: Babar

To help new Cambodian refugees settle in France, I became involved in numerous charities. Food has the power to nourish the body and the soul, and on a few occasions, it became my only resource to support people in difficulty.

There was a lady who had lost almost everything. Her nine children were either dead or had been placed in foster care. Life had become too overwhelming and she called me to say she wanted to end her misery.

I said, "You decide, this is your life. But before you do anything, please let me bring you a *babar*."

Babar is a simple dish, a rice congee cooked to a soft consistency. Easy to digest, it is renowned for its ability to bring comfort in times of need and is the food of choice for convalescent, sick or elderly people. Was it the *babar* or did she come round by herself? I will never really know, but this woman is still alive today.

Promoting and Sharing My Passion for Khmer Cuisine: P'lear Trey

As a teacher in vocational training and home economics, one of my main tasks was to train students in French culinary techniques. The teaching involved theoretical learning combined with practical hands-on experience in professionally equipped kitchens. Over the 20 years I spent in France, I gave countless demonstrations and cooking classes to my students.

My teaching skills were fully put to use when I was asked to promote Cambodian food. I held cooking classes and taught food hygiene in refugee camps in Thailand. I presented traditional dishes in various events organised by Cambodian charities in France.

For me, lime-marinated fish salad (*p'lear trey*), page 128, is the perfect dish to introduce Cambodian cuisine. The salad, made up of crunchy vegetables, aromatic herbs and spices, is balanced to bring out the flavours. It is in itself a testimony to Cambodia's fresh and fragrant cuisine. I have presented this dish many times, on a French television programme, *Cuisine des Autres* (*Cuisines of the World*), as well as to students at Le Cordon Bleu culinary school in London.

Becoming a Grandmother: Kroeung and Fish Amok

When she was expecting her first child, my daughter Kanika suddenly yearned to cook Cambodian dishes and go back to her roots. As it was with my mother and myself, her knowledge of cooking was almost non-existent as she had hardly set foot in the kitchen as a child. In our family, children are not involved in cooking and it is the duty of the parents to cook and feed their offspring.

Very few Cambodian cookbooks were available, much less any with recipes Kanika was used to eating at home. Recipes were passed down orally from mother to daughter, and the war broke down this verbal chain and with it, national pride and identity.

In the absence of a satisfactory cookbook, the idea of working together to carry on the tradition passing recipes on from mother to daughter, but in the written form, became very compelling for Kanika and myself.

Through researching, recording, cooking and photographing, we gradually reconnected with our culture, our families and with each other at a deeper level. The book had a unifying influence, drawing on the skills, enthusiasm and generosity of our friends and families.

My first attempt at producing a cookbook looked a bit like a school project and only three copies were printed although it had taken me a painstaking 10 years to produce it, working on my own. Working with my daughter and pooling our strengths, the project reached another level.

In February 2010, against all expectations, the French edition of our self-published cookbook won the prestigious Gourmand World Cookbook Awards, and was named the "*Best Asian Cuisine Cookbook in the World*".

The book now seems to have taken on a life of its own, gathering support from an incredible array of people. Just like a Cambodian freestyle dinner party, different people have taken responsibility for different parts, turning the whole thing into a feast. For all this amazing support and the joy of sharing the adventure with so many, I am immensely grateful every day.

Knowing that my children, grandchildren and others, will be able to prepare their own *kroeung* and fish *amok* and share it with their loved ones and friends using this book, gives me hope that Cambodia's beautiful culinary traditions will stay alive for future generations to enjoy.

Sorey Long

Notes

1. Cambodians write their family name before their first name.
2. Under the French protectorate (1863–1953), Cambodia was divided into 14 provinces (*khet*). Each province was sub-divided into districts (*srok*), and each district into communes (*khum*). The governor (*chauvay khet*) was an official appointed by the king and under French supervision, was in charge of governing the province (police, justice, education, public works etc). The head of the district (*chauvay srok*) held similar responsibilities but at district level.
3. Sapodilla is the fruit of a tree native to southern Mexico and Central America. There are many varieties, ranging from round to oval and from small to large. The skin is thin and smooth, turning yellow-brown when ripe. Inside, the flesh can be grainy in texture or smooth. Before it is ripe, the flesh is hard with an astringent taste. As it matures, the flesh becomes soft, with a sweet flavour and aroma, resembling that of a pear. Some fruit are seedless. Sapodilla is enjoyed unripe as a dip with *prahok* and is consumed ripe as a dessert.
4. Kapok refers to the pod of the kapok tree, native to south America. It is also known as the ceiba tree. The pod contains seeds surrounded by a whitish, fluffy fibre which is used as filling in mattresses and pillows.
5. *Mi bam pong* is crispy rice vermicelli, garnished with vegetables and pork.
6. Riel is the currency of Cambodia. At that time, 35 riels was equivalent to US$1.00
7. In Cambodia, the groom's family provides the dowry.
8. An adult education teacher was in charge of training villagers in rural areas. I specialised in home economics (cooking, nutrition, hygiene, weaving, sewing) and women specific training (sexual health and childcare). I also organised adult literacy courses.
9. *Saramann* paste (*saramann kroeung*), page 41 is made from finely ground spices and herbs such as cardamom, cinnamon, cloves, lemongrass, galangal and red chillies. *Saramann* paste is specifically used in *saramann* curry, page 111.
10. *Svay l'hong* is a variety of mango with a crunchy texture. It is commonly consumed nearly ripe with a dip.
11. Very few Cambodians owned refrigerators and food that required refrigeration such as cheese was not readily available. Today, many Cambodians own a refrigerator but most still favour fresh produce bought at the market daily.
12. The war had been raging since the beginning of 1970.
13. In 1968, aged 26, Long Botta was nominated Director of Secondary Education in Cambodia. A year later, he became the Secretary of State for Education. In 1973, he took on the post of High Commissioner for Youth and Sports, and in 1975, he was appointed Minister of Culture.
14. In Taluon, the village where my mother was born, long squashes (*tralach*) are first carved into flower shapes and then left to harden overnight in hydrolysed lime water. In the morning, they are thoroughly rinsed, drained and cooked in a large bronze pot with sugar. Once ready, they are transferred to a jar with the heavy syrup. They must be consumed within a week or two. Alternatively, once cooked, they can be left to dry in the sun until they are candied.
15. Béchamel sauce is made with butter, flour and milk, cooked slowly to a creamy texture.
16. I was appointed ETC (*Employés Techniques des Collectivités*, literally Technical Employees in Communities) teacher. ETC was a professional qualification offered in secondary schools. It prepared students for careers in nursing homes, nursery schools, catering and cleaning industries.
17. *Viennoiseries* are baked goods. They are eaten for breakfast or at teatime and include croissants, brioches, *pain au chocolat, pain aux raisins* and *chausson aux pommes*.

Khmer Culinary Traditions

Khmer culinary traditions mirror Cambodia's lushness in many ways. It draws on the abundance of fish, fruit and vegetables to create a cuisine which is always fragrant, and never excessively spicy.

The fertile banks of the Mekong River, Tonle Sap and Tonle Bassac provide an extraordinary variety of aromatic herbs, fruit and vegetables, while the lakes and rivers are home to hundreds of fish.

The famous *kroeung* paste for instance, made of lemongrass, galangal, turmeric, fingerroot (Chinese keys) and kaffir lime, is in itself, a testimony to Cambodia's abundance and diversity of ingredients.

Kroeung, aromatic herbs and *prahok* (fermented fish paste), subtly combined, bring out the flavours and give to the dishes a true taste of Cambodian food.

The most typical scents and flavours are, in my opinion, found in soups and salads.

The *samlar kâko* soup, page 60 for example, blends beautifully most of the ingredients Cambodia has to offer: fish, *kroeung*, *prahok*, winged beans, pea aubergines (eggplants/brinjals), green papayas, green bananas and fresh leaves (*sleuk bahs* and *sleuk m'rom*).

Salads invariably include a selection of fresh aromatic herbs (*t'chi*) which imparts a subtle fragrance.

Khmer people enjoy combining flavours such as sweet (*paem*), salty (*pray*), bitter (*l'evign*), sour (*chou*) and pungent (*chat*). They are particularly fond of the sweet-sour-salty combination found in many soups, sauces and dressings. In salads, sour notes come from unripe fruit such as green mangoes and papayas, and in stir-fries, the sweet-sour combination is the most common.

Certain flavours, however, are not to be mixed. In cooking as in love, bitter would not suffer any association with either sour or pungent. The painful result of mixing the two is eloquently described in a Cambodian love song which goes: "*Chivet khiom l'evign chou chat*" (My life is full of bitterness and sourness).

Key Ingredients

Rice

No meal is complete without rice

Rice is the staple of Cambodian cooking. An accompaniment to all meals, it is also used in its own right in many dishes, drinks and desserts. Cambodians commonly eat rice in different forms throughout a meal: plain, sticky, grilled, puffed or turned into noodles, flour and even alcohol.

Rice is not wasted and many dishes are made with leftover rice. Fried rice (*baï lign*), crispy rice cakes (*baï k'daing*), page 33 and chicken congee (*babar moan*), page 68 are among the most popular ones.

The importance of rice can be felt in the Cambodian language. Various forms of rice all have specific names such as:

Sreuv	Paddy rice, uncooked rice with the hull on
Angkâr	Uncooked rice, with the hull removed
Baï	Cooked rice
Leach	Uncooked glutinous rice that is sun-dried, then grilled and puffed
Ambok	Paddy rice, slightly cooked and flattened

The word for "eating" in Cambodian literally means "eating rice" and is expressed differently depending on the social context:

Soy krâya	for the Royal family
Eng cheunh pisâr baï	formal language
Hop baï	colloquial (in the countryside)
Gnam baï	colloquial (in cities, usually used by children)
Si baï	colloquial
Chhreas chhroim baï	slang

Proverbs reflect the importance of rice in Cambodia:

Rice is like a mother.

Standing straight, rice does not contain any grains, bowed down, it is ready to harvest. (This proverb is often quoted in relation to achieving success in life. One has to be humble and respectful; those who stand proud and superior are bound to fail.)

Leftover rice is still rice; likewise, a widow is still a woman.

Don't let an angry person do the washing up and don't let a hungry person cook rice.

Rice is planted when the soil is warm, courting is done when love gets strong.

The life of the villagers revolves around rice cultivation

In the countryside, most families live off rice cultivation. Rice growing is hard work, labour intensive and still uses very archaic methods, as depicted in Rithy Panh's film *Rice People* (*Neak Sre*). Villagers have established a system of mutual support to contend with the harshness of the work. Families pool resources at key times: transplanting, harvesting and threshing. These are special and joyous occasions where meals are shared and parties are held to celebrate a good harvest. For young men, this is the time to court young women.

Rice and Rites

Many rites, celebrations and ceremonies follow the cycle of rice cultivation. The most important one is the Sacred Furrow ceremony, also called the Royal Ploughing (Pithi Chrât Preah Nangkeal). It marks the beginning of the ploughing season and takes place on the fourth day of the new moon in May (the month of Visakh).

In bygone days, the king himself traced the first furrows in the sacred rice field, thus inaugurating the ploughing season. Today, the rite is performed by a man (King of Meakh) and a woman (Queen Me Hour) appointed by the king. After circling the rice field three times, the oxen pulling the Royal Plough are submitted to a divine test. Seven golden trays are presented to them, each containing different types of food and drink: paddy rice, beans, corn, sesame seeds, green grass, water and alcohol. The choice made by the oxen is interpreted as a good or bad omen for the coming year. If they choose the grains, it foretells an abundant harvest. If they drink water, rain and peace is expected. However, if they drink alcohol, then violence is feared.

Fish

Where there is water, there is fish (*mean teuk, mean trey*).

Cambodia is a country where fish are abundant, thanks to a unique hydrological phenomenon. During the rainy season, the powerful Mekong River, which runs

across the country from north to south, flows so heavily that it forces the water of the Tonle Sap River back and upstream into the great Tonle Sap Lake. The lake then turns into a gigantic overflow reservoir for the Mekong waters. Its surface area increases four to six-fold to 10,000–16,000 sq. km. As a result, hundreds of fish species have been found in the Tonle Sap Lake. It is a godsend for local fishermen, especially when the water levels fall back to normal. The myriad fish are trapped and fishermen enjoy bumper catches (see map, page 227).

Seafood comes mainly from the Kampot and Kampong Som provinces. They are either eaten locally or sold on the market in Phnom Penh. Due both to the heat and lack of refrigeration, fish cannot be kept fresh for very long. Cambodians therefore use traditional ways to preserve the fish by salting, sun-drying, smoking and fermenting. These traditional preservation techniques enable the preparation of *prahok* (fermented fish paste), *pha'ak* (a variation of *prahok*), fish sauce, dried and smoked fish. For all of these key ingredients, refer to the Glossary for details.

Kroeung

Along with *prahok*, *kroeung* is a very distinctive ingredient of Khmer cuisine. A fragrant paste made from lemongrass, galangal, turmeric, fingerroot (Chinese keys), kaffir lime, garlic and shallots, it gives a unique flavour and aroma to dishes. The ingredients are pounded in a mortar in a given order, patiently and meticulously. It is said that the fine qualities of a woman is associated with the way she prepares her *kroeung*.

Around a Khmer Table

Khmer people entertain with natural grace and warmth. To invite someone to share a meal is both an honour and a pleasure. Friends often drop by unannounced and

if the conversation lasts until mealtime, they will naturally be invited to stay on for the meal. Everyone sits around a low table called a *rean*. Women sit with their legs folded to the side while men sit cross-legged.

The hostess serves rice to the guests from a large bowl placed next to her. Dishes are rarely served in individual portions but everyone helps themselves from communal dishes. Courses do not follow a particular order and they tend to be brought to the table whenever they are ready, sometimes all at once, except for desserts. The notion of a starter or main course does not apply to Khmer meals. For a long time, Cambodians ate using their right hand, then gradually started to use spoons. Knives and forks are not required for a Cambodian meal, as the ingredients are typically cut into bite-size pieces before cooking. Chinese chopsticks are exclusively used for noodle stir-fries and noodle soups (*kuteav*).

Eating Habits

Eating habits differs between the countryside and cities.

Breakfast

In the countryside, breakfast is taken at home before dawn. It has to be filling and nourishing for a day's work in the field. Typically, villagers would have rice, plain or cooked as a soup, accompanied by dried or fried fish. Leftover rice can also be fried with a bit of lard and an egg.

In the cities, people have their breakfast later and may not eat at home but at restaurants or street stalls (*psa touch touch*). Breakfast is typically noodles, prepared either as a soup (*kuteav*) or stir-fried with vegetables and peanuts (*kuteav t'cha*). Plain rice, served either as a soup (*babar*) or stir-fried with meat (*baï moan, baï sach chrouk, baï pong tear*) is another popular favourite.

Lunch

Villagers take a break in the mid-morning. They carry their lunch in a small palm-leaf basket (*smok*) which typically consists of rice and dried fish wrapped in banana leaves. To season the fish, they use sour tamarind ground with chillies and salt, or wood apple (*krassaing*, see Glossary) pounded with garlic and salt. Lunch rarely includes dessert but fruit is taken in the afternoon.

In cities, the typical workday is from 7:00 am to 5:00 pm. Between noon and 2:00 pm, they typically have lunch followed by a short nap. Most offices do not provide canteens so people normally either go home for their meal or eat out. Lunch is a large meal for those who can afford it. It comprises several courses served with rice: fish or meat salad, stir-fry (*t'cha*) and soup. A fruit or coconut milk dessert ends the meal. Popular coconut milk desserts include bananas in coconut milk with tapioca (*chek k'tis*), page 166 and sticky rice in coconut milk with palm fruit (*babar tnaot*), page 163.

Snacks

Cambodians like eating throughout the day.

Among the sweet snacks, the most common are sticky rice and banana rolls (*nom an sam chek aing*), page 174 and banana fritters (*chek chienn*), page 170. There is also a delicious little cake made with rice steamed in coconut milk and sprinkled with freshly grated coconut (*akor*).

Among the savoury snacks, there is prawn fritters, half-hatched duck eggs, turtle eggs and grilled insects. Khmers are also very fond of sour fruit such as green mangoes and pungent ones such as green sapodillas (see Note 3, page 22). They are consumed with various dipping sauces, the two most popular ones being chopped *prahok* with palm sugar and chopped chilli in fish sauce.

Dinner

As night falls early, dinner is eaten in the early evening. In the villages, the evening meal generally consists of a sour soup made of fish, fruit and vegetables, such as young stems of lotus sour soup (*samlar m'chou krâ av chhouk*), page 64. In the cities, the evening meal is similar to lunch.

Drinks

In the countryside, villagers offer tea to their guests, especially to older people. Palm wine (*sra teuk tnaot chou*) is also very popular with Cambodians. To make palm wine, the sap of the sugar palm tree (*tnaot*) is collected, reduced and then fermented.

The largest production areas of palm wine are Takeo and Kompong Speu (see map, page 227). As the soil in these provinces is not very fertile, rice growing only takes place once a year, so farmers dedicate more time to palm wine production. Palm wine is generally served with grilled beef sausages, dried cuttlefish and vegetable pickles.

Villagers also enjoy drinking rice alcohol and a special wine called *sra thnam*. Made with macerated roots, this wine is believed to have medicinal properties especially for women after childbirth.

In towns, western influence on tastes is noticeable. Although people enjoy traditional drinks such as coconut juice, sugar cane juice and jasmine or lotus petal scented-water, beer, foreign wines and café frappé are also consumed regularly.

Traditional Khmer House and Kitchen

Traditional houses are made of wood and built on stilts. The walls and roof are made of palm leaves and bamboo. This mode of construction has many advantages. It protects its inhabitants from floods and keeps rats, snakes and other pests at bay. It also offers great protection against the heat of the sun. During the hot season, Cambodians take their afternoon naps in hammocks hung between stilts.

The space underneath the house can also be used as a storage area for farming or fishing tools and as a place to keep animals, such as cows, chickens and pigs. It is even occasionally turned into weaving or pottery workshops.

Inside the house, the space is divided into several rooms using wooden partitions. Typically, there would be a living room and one or two bedrooms. Furniture and storage are kept to a minimum. Simple rattan mats act both as beds and tables.

The kitchen is never located inside a traditional house. It is either underneath or, to avoid cooking fumes, behind the house. Kitchen floors are typically bare ground and again, like the rest of the house, very few pieces of furniture are found. A low wooden table (*rean*) located either in the kitchen or below the house is used interchangeably as a worktop, table, chair or even bed.

Meat is cut up on a wooden board (*chrugn*) with a large cleaver (*kambet paing tor*). Food is washed in a large aluminium container (*chan dèk*), using either rain or river water stored in large earthenware jars located beside the kitchen. To drain, a round bamboo basket (*kanchrèng*) is used.

Cooking is done in a wood-fired earthen kiln (*choeung krann*) resembling a large bucket. Cooking time is often quick and only a few utensils are required. One or two earthenware cooking pots, a wok and a kettle are ample. In contrast, the preparation of ingredients is time-consuming and requires specific utensils to peel, chop, grate, pound, grind and marinate.

To make *kroeung*, a stone mortar (*tbal bok*) is used. *Prahok*, lemon and tamarind juices are filtered through a bamboo strainer (*kân trung prahok*), while coconut is grated on a wooden and iron grater (*knâos kâos dông*). Rice flour is obtained by grinding the rice grains on a millstone (*kbal ken*). *Prahok*, *pha'ak*, coarse salt and pickles are preserved in small earthenware jars fitted with lids.

Basic Recipes

Steamed Rice

Baï Sâr

Fragrant rice, also known as jasmine rice, has a delicate fragrance and a soft, slightly sticky texture. Jasmine rice is available from Asian stores and mainstream groceries.

Preparation: Short • Cooking: 20 minutes • Serves 4

Long grain fragrant (jasmine) rice 200 g (7 oz), rinsed and drained

Water 200 ml (7 fl oz)

Cooking the traditional way

1. Put rice in a large saucepan, then cover with water. Bring water to the boil.
2. Reduce heat and simmer, uncovered, for about 10 minutes or until all the water has been absorbed.
3. Reduce heat to low, cover and cook for a further 5 minutes until rice is tender.

Cooking with an electric rice cooker

1. Place rice and water in a rice cooker.
2. Cook rice according to the manufacturer's instructions.

   Using an electric rice cooker is a simple and easy option. Although the rice cooker does not speed up the cooking process, it greatly reduces the cook's involvement.

NOTE

- Steamed rice is served at most meals with salads, stir-fries and soups. It can be stored for up to 3 days in the refrigerator. To reheat, sprinkle the rice with some water, then place in a steamer, microwave oven or in a saucepan over low heat.

TIPS

- Allow 50 g (1 2/3 oz) uncooked rice per person.
- As a rule of thumb, use the same quantity for water and rice. Traditionally, Cambodians used their fingertip to measure the right amount of water. The water line above the rice should be a fingertip deep or 2.5 cm (1 in).
- Choose a saucepan with a heavy base to prevent scorching on the bottom and a tight-fitting lid to keep the steam in.

Steamed Sticky Rice

Baï Damnoeub Chamhoy

Sticky or glutinous rice, requires a long soak in water before cooking. When cooked, the rice will approximately double in volume and be sticky and translucent.

Preparation: Long • Soaking: 3 hours • Cooking: 25 minutes • Serves 4

White sticky (glutinous) rice 500 g (1 lb 1 1/2 oz)

Salt 2 pinches

Coconut cream 200 ml (7 fl oz)

1. Rinse rice until water runs clear. Place in a large bowl. Add enough cold water to cover rice, then leave rice to soak for 3 hours. Drain, rinse thoroughly, then drain again.
2. Line a steamer basket with a piece of muslin (cheesecloth). Place rice on muslin and spread it out. This will help the grains cook more evenly.
3. Fill a wok one-third full with water and bring to the boil. Place the steamer with lid on over the wok. Steam for 25 minutes over high heat.
4. Dissolve salt in coconut cream, then sprinkle small amounts over rice frequently while it steams to moisten rice. Fluff the rice lightly each time with a fork to ensure coconut milk is absorbed evenly.
5. The rice is cooked when it becomes swollen, soft and translucent.

NOTE

- Black sticky rice is another type of sticky rice. Although so named, it is in reality dark purple. It has a richer and nuttier flavour than white sticky rice and is mainly used for desserts. White and black sticky rice are available from Asian stores.
- When steaming rice, keep the lid on the steamer to prevent heat from escaping and check that there is enough water in the wok.
- A bamboo steamer works better than a stainless steel one, as the former will impart a subtle flavour to the dish cooked in it.
- Sticky rice can be stored for up to 2 days in the refrigerator. To reheat, sprinkle some water over the rice and place in a steamer or microwave oven.

Crispy Rice Cakes

Baï K'daing

Crispy rice cakes were originally a snack made from leftovers. Instead of discarding rice that often stuck to the bottom of the pot, it was carefully scraped off, dried out under the sun for several days before being deep-fried into crispy rice cakes.

Preparation: Short • Drying: Several days • Cooking: 25 minutes • Makes about 20 rice cakes

Long grain fragrant (jasmine) rice 50 g (1 2/3 oz), rinsed and drained

Cooking oil for deep-frying 500 ml (16 fl oz / 2 cups)

1. In a large and heavy nonstick saucepan, cook rice using the traditional method (page 32). Let it cook longer than usual, for an additional 15 minutes over low heat.
2. Scoop out steamed rice. With a wooden spatula, carefully remove the rice stuck at the bottom of the saucepan. This is known as the rice crust. With a pair of scissors, cut the rice crust into small rectangles about 2 x 3 cm (3/4 x 1 in).
3. Dry out rice pieces in a well-ventilated area until hard and fully dry. This may take several days.
4. To make crispy rice cakes, heat oil in a wok. When the oil is very hot, deep-fry dried rice pieces until crisp but not golden brown. Remove rice cakes quickly with a mesh strainer. Drain on kitchen paper.
5. Serve immediately with *nataing* sauce (page 148).

NOTE

- For this recipe, do not use a rice cooker as it rarely leaves any rice crust at the bottom.
- For colder and more humid climates, instead of leaving the rice crust to dry in the sun, dry them out in a very slow oven.
- Dried rice can be stored in an airtight container for several months and deep-fried when needed.

Roasted Ground Rice

Angkâr Lign

Roasted ground rice adds flavour and texture when sprinkled on salads and dishes such as *samlar kâko* soup (page 60).

Preparation: Short • Soaking: 1 hour • Cooking: 5–10 minutes

Long grain fragrant (jasmine) rice a handful

1. Soak rice in cold water for 1 hour. Rinse thoroughly, then drain.
2. Dry-roast rice in a wok over medium heat. Stir frequently using a wooden spoon until rice is golden brown.
3. Remove rice and allow to cool. Grind grains to a fairly coarse powder, using a mortar and pestle or a food processor.

NOTE

- Roasted rice can be stored for several weeks in an airtight container.

Fried Chopped Garlic

Ktim Sâr Bâmpong

Fried chopped garlic and the resulting fragrant oil are used as a garnish, mainly for soups, to give texture and flavour.

Preparation: Short • Cooking: 5 minutes

Garlic 1 head

Cooking oil 200 ml (7 fl oz)

1. Separate head of garlic into individual cloves. Peel and finely chop cloves.
2. Heat oil in a wok and fry garlic over low heat. Stir frequently using a wooden spoon, until garlic is golden and crispy. Remove from wok and allow to cool.

Variation

Fried Sliced Garlic

- The cloves are thinly sliced, then fried until golden and crispy. They are used in salad dressings or sprinkled on top of dishes as garnish.

Fried Sliced Shallots (*Ktim Krâhâm Bâmpong*)

- Peel and finely slice shallots, then brown in oil over low heat. They are used as garnish to give taste and texture to soups, salads and dressings.

NOTE

- Fried garlic and shallots and garlic oil can be stored in an airtight container for 2 to 3 days.

Chicken Stock

Teuk Soup

Cambodian cooking relies heavily on stocks. Chicken stock is used as a base for various soups and fondues. It is also used to enhance the flavour of stir-fries and steamed dishes. Ready made stock is available from supermarkets, but try making your own stock, if time permits.

Preparation: Short • Cooking: 1 hour •
Resting: 30 minutes • Makes 2.5 litres (80 fl oz / 10 cups)

Chicken bones 1 kg (2 lb 3 oz), skin and fat removed

Cold water 3 litres (96 fl oz / 12 cups)

Onion 1, peeled and coarsely chopped

Coarse salt 1 tsp

1. Rinse chicken bones, put into a large pot and cover with water. Bring to the boil.
2. Discard water, drain bones and place them in another pot. Add cold water, onion and coarse salt. Simmer for 1 hour, uncovered.
3. Remove from heat and leave to stand for 30 minutes. Remove chicken bones and strain stock.

NOTE

- Stock takes a long time to cook, so make a huge batch at one go.
- Unused stock can be kept refrigerated for up to 3 days or frozen for up to 3 months. When left in the refrigerator for several hours, a thin layer of fat appears on the surface of stock. Scoop out and discard the fat before reheating stock.
- If freezing stock, store in small quantities in freezer bags or in ice cube trays.

Vegetable Stock

Teuk Soup Banlè

Vegetable stock is a good substitute for chicken stock. Packed with vitamins and minerals, vegetable stock is easy to make and is used as a base for many soups and fondues. It enhances the flavour of stir-fries and steamed dishes. Make your own stock, if time permits.

Preparation: Average • Cooking: 40 minutes • Resting: 30 minutes • Makes 2.5 litres (80 fl oz / 10 cups)

White radish 1, peeled and cubed

Carrots 2, peeled and cubed

Celery stalks 3, cut into sticks

Onion 1, peeled and chopped coarsely

Coriander (cilantro) seeds 1 tsp

Black peppercorns 1/2 tsp

Water 3 litres (96 fl oz / 12 cups)

Coarse salt 1 tsp

1. Combine all ingredients in a large pot.
2. Simmer for 30 minutes, uncovered.
3. Remove from heat and leave to stand for 30 minutes. Strain stock.

NOTE

- Stock takes a long time to cook so make a huge batch at one go. Refrigerate unused stock for up to 3 days or freeze for up to 3 months. Store in small quantities in freezer bags or ice cube trays.
- The white radish can be substituted with 2 turnips.

Tamarind Juice

Teuk Ampil

The tamarind tree produces light brown pods that contain large shiny seeds covered with a dark brown pulp. This pulp can be very sweet to very sour, depending on the variety and maturity of the tamarind. For the recipes in this book, choose sour tamarind.

Using fresh tamarind pods

1. In soup recipes, add the whole tamarind pods to the pot with the other ingredients.
2. Cook soup by following recipe instructions.
3. When cooking is almost over, transfer the tamarind pods to a large bowl. Mash with a fork, pressing against solids (pods, fibres and seeds) to extract as much juice as possible. Dilute with a ladle of hot soup stock. Strain juice and discard solids. Use juice to season soup.

Using tamarind pulp

1. Tamarind pulp comes in soft rectangular blocks wrapped in plastic. In Cambodia, they come in balls of around 100 g (3 1/2 oz) each.
2. To extract tamarind juice from pulp, place the pulp in a bowl and add hot water. Leave to soak for 10 minutes.
3. Use your fingers to knead and dissolve pulp. Strain juice and discard any seeds and fibre. Use juice as required in recipe.

NOTE

- Tamarind juice is used as a souring agent for soups and sauces. The traditional way of extracting the juice is to use fresh pods or pulp. This takes time so, for convenience, opt for tamarind concentrate or powder. Tamarind pods, pulp and concentrate or powder are available in Asian and Indian markets. Alternatively, substitute with lime juice.
- In all recipes using tamarind juice, add the juice gradually, doing a taste test after each addition until the right flavour is achieved.

Coconut Milk

K'tis Dông

Coconut milk gives a creamy and mildly sweet taste, and adds smoothness to curries, soups, salads and desserts. The clear liquid found inside a coconut is not coconut milk but coconut water. Coconut milk is the extract of freshly grated coconut. Extracting coconut milk takes time, so for convenience, substitute with canned unsweetened coconut milk. Leave the canned coconut milk to stand and you will see a layer of thick cream float to the top, with a more watery layer of milk at the bottom. Some recipes use both the creamy and the more liquid parts of the coconut milk while others use only the creamy part.

Preparation: Long • Makes about 200 ml (7 fl oz)

Well-matured coconut 1 whole

Lukewarm water 200 ml (7 fl oz)

1. Finely hand-grate coconut flesh using a coconut grater.
2. Line a large bowl with a piece of muslin (cheesecloth). Place freshly grated coconut on muslin and pour over lukewarm water.
3. Gather up the edges of muslin and squeeze tightly to extract coconut milk (or first milk). Leave milk to stand in the refrigerator.
4. Coconut cream is the thick white part that separates and rises to the top of the thinner liquid or coconut milk.

Dry-roasted Grated Coconut

Dông Lign

Dry-roasted grated coconut adds a crunchy texture and a nutty flavour when it is used on salads as a garnish. Dry-roasted coconut also pairs well with curries. It is a key ingredient in *saramann kroeung*, the paste used in *saramann* curry (page 111). When possible, use freshly grated coconut. It is tastier and crunchier. Otherwise, substitute with frozen grated coconut or desiccated coconut (also called dried shredded coconut) found in Indian and Asian stores. For desiccated coconut, be careful to buy the unsweetened kind as the sweetened type, most commonly available in the baking section of grocery stores, is not suitable for this recipe.

Preparation: Average • Cooking: 15 minutes

Well-matured coconut 1 whole or 500 g (1 lb 1½ oz) frozen grated coconut or unsweetened desiccated coconut

1. If using a whole coconut, finely hand-grate coconut flesh using a coconut grater.
2. In a heavy-based wok or frying pan, dry-roast grated coconut or desiccated coconut over low heat. Stir constantly until the shreds are dry, aromatic and golden brown.
3. Allow dry-roasted grated coconut to cool completely. Store in the refrigerator in an airtight container for up to 1 week.

Omelette for Garnish

Porn Tear Chienn

Sliced into thin strips, omelette is the perfect garnish for stir-fried rice or stir-fried noodles. When cooking omelette, use the freshest eggs you can find. A nonstick 15-cm (6-in) omelette or pancake pan is ideal for creating the perfect omelette.

Preparation: Short • Cooking: 10 minutes • Makes about 4 omelettes

Eggs 2

Salt a pinch

Cooking oil 1 tsp

1. Beat eggs into a bowl and season with salt.
2. Heat oil in pan over medium heat. Pour in a small quantity of beaten eggs into the centre of the pan. Working quickly, tilt pan to spread eggs evenly over the base, like a thin pancake. When golden and crispy, flip the omelette over and cook the other side. Remove from heat.
3. Repeat steps until there is no more beaten eggs. Roll up tightly each omelette. Trim ends and cut into thin slices.

Kroeungs

Kroeung is a smooth paste of herbs and spices pounded together. The six key ingredients are lemongrass, galangal, kaffir lime zest, turmeric, garlic and shallots. *Kroeung* is distinctively Khmer, giving a unique and aromatic flavour to many Khmer dishes such as stir-fries, sour soups, grilled meat, steamed meals and curries. There are five types of *kroeung*. These are yellow *kroeung*, green *kroeung*, red *kroeung*, *k'tis kroeung* and *saramann kroeung*.

The names of yellow, green and red *kroeung* are based on the colour given by a particular ingredient used in the paste. Turmeric lends its distinctive bright orange colour to yellow *kroeung*; lemongrass leaves give colour to green *kroeung*; and red *kroeung* gets its colour from the addition of dried red chillies.

Yellow *kroeung* is used in many recipes, while *saramann kroeung* is specifically used for *saramann* curry (page 111).

Quantities, freshness of the ingredients and the method of preparing and pounding the ingredients are essential to achieving good *kroeung*.

Firstly, it is very important to know how to cut each ingredient to ensure it will reduce to a smooth paste when pounded. Ingredients should be peeled and sliced thinly. They should then be added gradually and in a given order for pounding.

Use a stone mortar and pestle to hand-pound. Always start with the hardest ingredients which will require more time for pounding such as lemongrass, galangal and kaffir lime zest. This can be followed by turmeric. Finish with garlic and shallots which are more watery.

Making *kroeung* is a long process which involves hand-pounding to bring out the flavours more fully. In Cambodia, *kroeung* is prepared daily and used fresh. For convenience, use a food processor and make larger quantities without adding garlic and shallots. Freeze the *kroeung* in ice cube trays, then thaw the required amount when needed and pound together with fresh garlic and shallots.

Yellow Kroeung

Kroeung Samlar M'chou

Yellow *kroeung* is used in soups, fish *amok* (page 74), grilled meat, stir-fries and dips. This *kroeung* uses the stalks of lemongrass.

Preparation: Long • Makes about 250 g (9 oz)

Lemongrass stalks 200 g (7 oz), ends trimmed, outer layers removed and finely chopped

Galangal 1 Tbsp, peeled and chopped

Kaffir lime zest 1 tsp

Turmeric 1 tsp, peeled and chopped

Garlic 5 cloves, peeled and chopped

Shallots 2, peeled and chopped

1. Prepare all ingredients for pounding. Remember to add ingredients gradually and in the listed order.
2. Using a mortar and pestle, pound together lemongrass, galangal and kaffir lime zest. Add turmeric and repeat to pound. Finish with garlic and shallots. Pound into a fine paste. Alternatively, use a food processor.

Green Kroeung

Kroeung Prâhoeur

Green *kroeung* is used in *samlar kâko* soup (page 60), stuffed chicken wings (page 102) and rice vermicelli with green sauce (page 156). This paste uses lemongrass leaves which have a stronger flavour than the stalks and give their colour to this *kroeung*.

Preparation: Long • Makes about 350 g (12 oz)

Lemongrass leaves 300 g (11 oz), finely chopped

Kaffir lime zest 1 tsp

Turmeric 1 tsp, peeled and chopped

Fingerroot (Chinese keys) 2 Tbsp, peeled and chopped

Garlic 5 cloves, peeled and chopped

Shallots 2, peeled and chopped

1. Prepare all ingredients for pounding. Remember to add ingredients gradually and in the listed order.
2. Using a mortar and pestle, pound together the first four ingredients, then add garlic and shallots. Pound paste until smooth. Alternatively, use a food processor.

Red Kroeung

Kroeung Samlar Cari

This *kroeung* is used to make chicken curry (page 96).

Preparation: Long • Cooking: A few minutes • Makes about 100 g (3½ oz)

Coriander (cilantro) seeds 1 Tbsp

Cumin seeds 1 tsp

Lemongrass stalks 2 Tbsp, finely chopped

Galangal 1 Tbsp, peeled and finely chopped

Kaffir lime zest 1 tsp

Dried red chillies 4, soaked until soft, drained, seeded and finely chopped

Turmeric ½ tsp, peeled and chopped

Garlic 10 cloves, peeled and chopped

Shallots 5, peeled and chopped

Prawn (shrimp) paste 1 tsp

1. Dry-roast over low heat all the ingredients except for prawn paste.
2. Remember to pound ingredients gradually and in the listed order. Using a mortar and pestle, start by pounding coriander and cumin seeds. Continue to add the other ingredients gradually, adding garlic and shallots last. Pound into a fine paste. Alternatively, use a food processor.
3. Mix in prawn paste.

K'tis Kroeung

Kroeung Samlar K'tis

This *kroeung* pairs well with soups and grilled fish.

Preparation: Long • Makes about 150 g (5⅓ oz)

Lemongrass stalks 100 g (3½ oz), finely chopped

Galangal 1 Tbsp, peeled and finely chopped

Kaffir lime zest 1 tsp

Dried red chillies 4, soaked, drained, seeded and finely chopped

Turmeric 1 tsp, peeled and chopped

Fingerroot (Chinese keys) 1 tsp, peeled and sliced

Garlic 10 cloves, peeled and chopped

Shallots 5, peeled and chopped

Prawn (shrimp) paste 1 tsp

1. Place all the ingredients, except for prawn paste, in a mortar and pound until smooth. Alternatively, use a food processor.
2. Mix in prawn paste.

Saramann Kroeung

Kroeung Samlar Saramann

This paste is specifically for *saramann* curry (page 111).

Preparation: Long • Cooking: A few minutes •
Makes about 150 g ($5^1/_3$ oz)

Dry-roasted grated coconut (page 36) 100 g ($3^1/_2$ oz)

Prawn (shrimp) paste 2 tsp

Coarse salt 2 tsp

Dry spices

Green cardamoms 3

Cinnamon stick 5 cm (2 in), broken into small pieces

Star anise 3, gently cracked

Cloves 4

Coriander (cilantro) seeds 2 Tbsp

Cumin seeds 2 tsp

Herbs and other spices

Coriander (cilantro) root 1 tsp, finely grated

Lemongrass stalks 4 Tbsp, finely chopped

Galangal 3 tsp, peeled and finely chopped

Kaffir lime zest 1 tsp

Dried red chillies 5, soaked, drained, seeded and chopped

Turmeric $^1/_2$ tsp, peeled and chopped

Garlic 15 cloves, peeled and chopped

Shallots 5, peeled and chopped

1. Place dry spices in a pan and dry-roast over low heat. Keep tossing constantly to prevent burning, until spices give off a rich aroma. Bruise cardamoms, remove seeds and discard pods. Grind, then sift spices. Set aside.
2. In the same pan, dry-roast herbs and other spices until they release a warm aroma. Remove from heat and place in a mortar with dry-roasted grated coconut. Pound into a smooth paste. Alternatively, use a food processor.
3. Mix in prawn paste, salt and ground spices.

Condiments, Dressings & Sauces

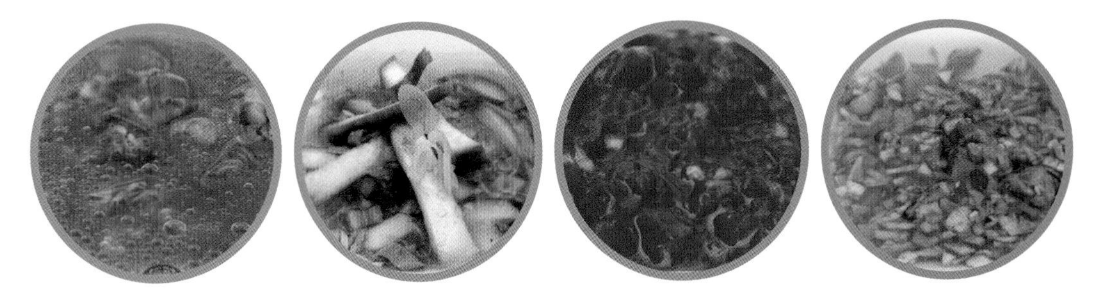

Condiments, dressings and sauces are essential in Cambodian cuisine. Their distinctive flavours enhance dishes and whet the appetite. They are varied because a wide range of ingredients and souring agents are used. Little oil or fat is used in their preparation, making them very healthy. Typical souring agents are palm vinegar, lime juice and tamarind. Fresh, unripe fruit can also act as a souring agent. Fresh tamarind, wood apple (*krassaing*), unripe *sandan* (*Garcinia cochinchinensis*) are common, together with green mangoes. Some preparations use no souring agent at all, such as the sauce made with salted soy beans and finely pounded young ginger root.

Condiments, dressings and sauces are prepared depending on what is in season. In March and April, when green mangoes start to become available, the fruit is chopped, seasoned with fish sauce, sugar and chillies, then used as a dressing with grilled fish. From July, fresh tamarind or *sandan*, pounded with a little water, salt and chillies, make the perfect accompaniment to grilled fish. For lamb or beef, the taste of the condiments and sauces will be more pronounced, to balance the stronger flavour of the meat. This is achieved by using ingredients such garlic, galangal and *prahok* (*prahok* dipping sauce, page 45). Achieving the right balance of seasoning requires some experimenting. For instance, fish sauce, because of its strong salty flavour, is generally added last. It can easily upset the balance of the seasoning, so add in small amounts and adjust according to taste. In this chapter, the measures indicated will give you the scope to try and experiment.

Sticky Rice Dipping Sauce

Teuk Trey Paem

This sauce goes well with summer rolls (page 52) and grilled meat patties (page 112). The consistency of this sauce should be quite thick.

Soaking: Long • Preparation: Short

White sticky (glutinous) rice 5 Tbsp, rinsed, soaked for 3 hours, then drained

Water 1litre (32 fl oz / 4 cups)

Palm sugar 2 Tbsp

Salt 2 pinches

Palm vinegar sauce (page 44) as needed

Hoisin sauce as needed

Unsalted peanuts 2 Tbsp, roasted and ground

Carrot 1, peeled and grated

Fresh bird's eye chillies 2, seeded and sliced

1. Place sticky rice in a pot and cover with 500 ml (16 fl oz / 2 cups) water. Bring to the boil.
2. Reduce heat to low and gradually pour in remaining water. Leave to simmer until all the water has been absorbed.
3. Season with palm sugar and salt. Cook for another 5 minutes, then remove from heat. Allow to cool before use.
4. In individual dipping bowls, place 2 Tbsp palm vinegar sauce, 2 Tbsp sticky rice and top with 1/2 tsp hoisin sauce. Sprinkle with peanuts, grated carrot and sliced bird's eye chillies.

Lime Juice Sauce

Teuk Trey Krauch Chmar

This is the perfect dressing for salads, fish and seafood. To extract lime juice easily, roll the limes firmly on a kitchen worktop before cutting them.

Preparation: Short • Makes about 150 ml (5 fl oz)

Fresh bird's eye chilli (optional) 1

Coriander (cilantro) roots 3, grated and finely chopped

Garlic 1 clove, peeled

Sugar 1 Tbsp

Lime juice 5 Tbsp

Fish sauce 3 Tbsp

Water 2 Tbsp

Salt to taste

1. Pound together chilli, if using, coriander roots, garlic and sugar.
2. Add lime juice, fish sauce and water. Mix well. Season to taste with salt.

Palm Vinegar Sauce

Teuk Trey Leay Nung Teuk Kmès Teuk Tnaot

This is a basic sauce used as a dip for summer rolls (page 52), rice and coconut pancakes and crispy rice pancakes. For a more varied texture and flavour, add peanuts, grated carrot, garlic and shallots.

Preparation: Short • Cooking: 5 minutes •
Makes about 1.5 litres (48 fl oz / 6 cups)

Water 750 ml (24 fl oz / 3 cups)

Sugar 200 g (7 oz)

Palm vinegar or white wine vinegar 250 ml (8 fl oz / 1 cup)

Fish sauce 250 ml (8 fl oz / 1 cup)

Garnish

Carrot 1, peeled and julienned

Garlic 2 cloves, peeled and julienned

Shallots 1, peeled and julienned

Unsalted peanuts as desired, roasted and ground

1. Put water and sugar in a saucepan. Bring to the boil, then remove from heat. Add palm vinegar and fish sauce. Allow to cool.
2. To serve, put sauce in individual dipping bowls. Sprinkle with carrot, garlic, shallots and peanuts.

NOTE

- If the taste of fish sauce is too strong for you, substitute with 2½ tsp salt.
- The sauce can be stored without the garnish in a sealed glass jar. Refrigerate for up to 2 months. Bring the sauce to room temperature before serving.

Peanut and Galangal Sauce

Teuk Trey Bok Sandek Dey Nung Romdéng

This sauce goes well with grilled fish.

Preparation: Short • Cooking: 5 minutes •
Makes about 250 ml (8 fl oz / 1 cup)

Garlic 2 cloves, unpeeled

Shallots 2, unpeeled

Galangal 2 slices, peeled

Unsalted peanuts 2 Tbsp, roasted and ground

Coriander (cilantro) root 1 tsp, grated and sliced

Fresh bird's eye chilli (optional) 1

Palm vinegar sauce (page 44) 250 ml (8 fl oz / 1 cup)

1. Dry-roast garlic and shallots in a pan over medium heat until skins are black. The inside should be soft throughout. Allow to cool, then peel the skins.
2. Using the same pan, dry-roast galangal.
3. Place dry-roasted ingredients in a mortar together with peanuts, coriander and chilli, if using. Pound into a fine paste. Alternatively, use a food processor.
4. Stir in palm vinegar sauce.

Tamarind Dipping Sauce

Teuk Trey Ampil Tom

This dip is perfect with grilled fish. Add tamarind juice gradually, tasting after each addition as the sourness of tamarind depends on the variety and the maturity of the pods.

Preparation: Short • Cooking: 10 minutes • Serves 4

Cooking oil 1 Tbsp

Minced pork 100 g (3$^1/_2$ oz)

Tamarind juice made using 100 g (3$^1/_2$ oz) tamarind pulp and 750 ml (24 fl oz / 3 cups) hot water and strained (page 35)

Palm sugar 3 Tbsp

Fish sauce 4 Tbsp

Fried sliced garlic (page 34) 1 Tbsp

Fried sliced shallots (page 34) 2 Tbsp

Fresh bird's eye chillies (optional) 1 tsp, seeded and sliced

1. Heat oil in a wok over medium heat. Add pork and stir vigorously to prevent pork from sticking together in lumps. Add tamarind juice, palm sugar and fish sauce. Toss gently to mix well. Continue to stir-fry until pork is cooked.
2. Remove from heat and adjust seasoning to taste. Sprinkle with fried garlic, shallots and chillies, if using.

Prahok Dipping Sauce

Teuk Prahok

This dip enhances meat dishes such as roasted lamb or grilled beef.

Preparation: Short • Cooking: 10 minutes • Makes about 150 ml (5 fl oz)

Garlic 5 cloves, unpeeled

Shallots 5, unpeeled

Galangal 3 thin slices, peeled

Prahok 1 Tbsp, wrapped and roasted in banana leaves

Sugar 1 Tbsp

Lemon juice extracted from 3 lemons

Water about 100 ml (3$^1/_2$ fl oz)

Salt to taste

Garnish

Asian round aubergines (eggplants/brinjals), green variety 500 g (1 lb 1$^1/_2$ oz), julienned

Lemongrass stalks 2, finely sliced

Sawtooth coriander 1 bunch, sliced in fine strips

Fresh bird's eye chillies (optional) 2, seeded and sliced

1. Dry-roast garlic and shallots in a pan over medium heat until skins are black. The inside should be soft throughout. Allow to cool, then peel the skins.
2. Using the same pan, dry-roast galangal.
3. Place galangal, garlic and shallots in a mortar and pound. Transfer to a mixing bowl. Add *prahok* and sugar. Stir in lemon juice and enough water to get a thick sauce.
4. Garnish with aubergines, lemongrass, sawtooth coriander and chillies, if using. Season to taste with salt.

Red Pepper Dressing

Chruok M'tés

This dressing is used as a garnish for pickled vegetables. The main ingredient is the long and narrow bull's horn pepper, which is delicious fresh or roasted. If unavailable, use red capsicum (bell pepper).

Preparation: Short • Cooking: 15 minutes • Makes about 100 ml (3½ fl oz)

Bull's horn red peppers 500 g (1 lb 1½ oz)

Water 2 litres (64 fl oz / 8 cups)

Garlic 1 head, peeled and finely chopped

Palm vinegar 3 Tbsp

Fish sauce 3 Tbsp

Sugar 3 Tbsp

Salt 1 tsp

1. Trim and discard stalk ends of peppers. Using the tip of a sharp knife, cut each pepper in half lengthwise. Scrape off white pith and seeds.
2. Put water in a saucepan and bring to the boil. Add peppers and cook for 15 minutes. Remove from heat, drain and slice thinly.
3. In a mixing bowl, combine peppers and remaining ingredients.
4. Store sauce in a sealed glass jar and refrigerate until needed. It should keep for several days. Bring the sauce to room temperature before serving.

Pickled Vegetables

Chruok Chhamros

Crunchy in texture and visually appealing, pickled vegetables go well with appetisers and grilled meats. As a serving suggestion, skewer the pickled vegetables with toothpicks, then stick them into a pomelo and serve with fried spring rolls. It is always a big hit at parties. For this recipe, try other vegetables such as cauliflower, cut into florets, white radish and nearly ripe papaya.

Preparation: Long • Standing: A few days • Serves 4 to 6

Water 750 ml (24 fl oz / 3 cups)

Coarse salt 2½ Tbsp

Sugar 200 g (7 oz)

White wine vinegar 250 ml (8 fl oz / 1 cup)

Carrots 2, peeled and thinly sliced

Green cabbage ¼ head, cut into 2 x 4-cm (1 x 1½-in) rectangles

Cucumber ½, cored and cut into finger-lengths

Long beans or French beans 3, cut into short lengths

Ginger 1 thumb-size knob, peeled and julienned

Garlic 2 cloves, peeled and sliced in half lengthwise

1. Put water, salt and sugar in a large saucepan. Bring to the boil, then remove from heat. Add vinegar. Cool to room temperature.
2. Combine vegetables, ginger and garlic and pack into a glass jar with a tight-fitting lid. Pour in pickling liquid, pressing vegetables down to make sure they are well submerged.
3. Seal jar and leave to stand for a few days before serving. Allow 2 days in summer and 3–4 days in winter. No refrigeration is required. Once the jar is open, store in the refrigerator.

Starters

Fried Spring Rolls Nom Chienn

In this recipe, fried spring rolls are served as a starter with vegetables and dipping sauce. Alternatively, to serve spring rolls as appetisers, use brick pastry sheets instead of rice paper wrappers. This will make the rolls crisper and lighter. Served with pickled vegetables (page 46), they are perfect for cocktail parties.

Preparation: Long • Cooking: 20 minutes • Serves 4 to 6

Rice paper (spring roll) wrappers 1 package, 15-cm (6-in) rounds or brick pastry sheets (*feuilles de brick*) 1 package, small, square sheets, thawed

Warm water to soften rice paper wrappers

Oil for deep-frying 500 ml (16 fl oz / 2 cups)

Palm vinegar sauce (page 44) as needed

Filling

Mung bean vermicelli (glass noodles) a handful, soaked in lukewarm water for 10 minutes to soften, drained and cut in 2-cm (1-in) lengths

Dried black fungus 1 Tbsp, soaked in lukewarm water for 20 minutes to soften, drained, stemmed and sliced thinly

Minced pork 300 g (11 oz)

Carrot 1, peeled, grated and excess water squeezed out using your palms

Onion 1 small, peeled and chopped finely

Salt 2 pinches

1. Prepare filling. In a large bowl, combine vermicelli, black fungus, minced pork, carrot and onion. Season with salt. Mix until evenly combined.
2. To make spring rolls, dip a sheet of rice paper in a shallow dish of warm water. Lift it up straight away and place on a clean moist tea towel on a flat surface. Do not leave rice paper to soak as it will tear easily when rolled. Skip this step if using brick pastry sheets.
3. On the bottom third of rice paper/pastry sheet, spread 2 Tbsp filling. Fold rice paper/pastry sheet over filling and roll up tightly. Fold in opposite ends towards the centre and over the filling, then continue rolling (see technique, page 204).
4. Repeat steps 2 and 3 until filling is used up.
5. Heat oil and deep-fry spring rolls over medium heat until golden brown and crisp. Remove. Drain well.
6. To eat, wrap warm spring rolls in lettuce leaves, tuck in slices of cucumber and fresh aromatic herbs (sweet basil and mint). Dip in palm vinegar sauce.

Variation

- Substitute pork with chicken breasts and/or prawns (shrimps). Choose vegetables for filling depending on your taste and which vegetables are in season. Try bean sprouts, green cabbage, taro and potatoes.

NOTE

- To secure the rolls more firmly, make a paste of flour and water. In a small saucepan, stir 1 tsp flour with 4 Tbsp water over medium heat until thickened. Allow to cool, then brush a little paste on the final edge of rice paper/pastry sheet to seal the roll.
- Spring rolls take a long time to prepare, so you may want to make a larger quantity and freeze the excess uncooked spring rolls. Deep-fry the frozen spring rolls straight from the freezer.

Rice and Coconut Pancakes Nom Krourk

These pancakes are a very popular street snack, prepared and cooked on the spot by street vendors. They are sold hot with a dipping sauce. In bygone days, to attract customers, the street vendors would cry out: "*Nom krourk chralourk teuk trey, Nom mouy sonn bey, Nom mouy roye m'pey, Tlay pon mann?*" ("Rice and coconut pancakes dipped in fish sauce, One pancake costs just 0.3 cents, For 120 pancakes, how much would that cost?")

Nom krourk are made from a mixture of rice flour and coconut milk. The batter is poured into a hot *nom krourk* pan, placed directly over a charcoal fire.

The *nom krourk* pan is round and made of cast-iron or terracotta, with hemispherical indentations (holes) about the size of golf balls. Substitute with an *ebelskiver* or a *poffertjes* pan (used to make Danish and Dutch pancakes respectively), as they are similar to the *nom krourk* pan, only with fewer and larger indentations. These cast-iron pans work fine on gas, electric or induction hobs.

Preparation: Short • Cooking: 20 minutes

Rice flour 500 g (1 lb 1 1/2 oz)

Coconut milk 200 ml (7 fl oz)

Coconut cream 200 ml (7 fl oz), set aside 3 Tbsp for topping

Water as needed

Salt 2 pinches

Fresh chives 1 Tbsp, snipped

Cooking oil 100 ml (3 1/2 fl oz), to grease pan

Potato 1/2, unpeeled, pricked on the skin side with a fork, to make a potato brush

Palm vinegar sauce (page 44) 250 ml (8 fl oz / 1 cup)

Chilli sauce to taste

1. To make batter, place rice flour in a large mixing bowl. Gradually pour in coconut milk, coconut cream and water and whisk until smooth. Add salt and sprinkle with chives.
2. Heat *nom krourk* pan over medium heat and when hot, grease holes with a little oil, using the potato brush. Pour enough batter into each hole to fill it up. Cover the pan with a lid and cook over medium heat until pancakes are lightly golden brown and crisp around the edge. Remove using a flexible spatula. Re-grease the pan before making the next batch.
3. Serve pancakes hot with palm vinegar sauce for dipping and topped with coconut cream and chilli sauce.

NOTE

- The amount of water required to make the batter will depend on the quality of the rice flour. You may need to experiment. New rice (*angkâr sreuv tmei*) or rice that has just been harvested, is more glutinous and tender in texture than old rice (*angkâr sreuv tch'has*). Therefore, flour made from new rice will make a softer *nom krourk*, so less water should be added. Flour from old rice will make a rather dry and hard *nom krourk*, so in this case, a little more water is needed.

Summer Rolls Nom Kreab Toteuk

Summer rolls are delicious rice paper rolls filled with crunchy raw vegetables, cold vermicelli, prawns and aromatic herbs. Light and refreshing yet substantial, these rolls require very little cooking. They are very popular served as a starter or light meal.

There are many variations to this recipe. Try adding or replacing bean sprouts with grated carrots. Substitute prawns with pre-cooked shredded pork fillet or chicken. Alternatively, choose the vegetarian option by using only vegetables.

Preparation: 20 minutes • Cooking: A few minutes • Makes 18 rolls

Rice paper (spring roll) wrappers 18 sheets, each 15-cm (6-in) round

Warm water to soften rice paper wrappers

Filling

Round lettuce or Batavia lettuce 1 head, rinsed, pat- or spun-dry

Fresh rice vermicelli a handful

Cucumber 1/2, julienned

Bean sprouts 2 handfuls, tailed

Fresh aromatic herbs an assorted bunch of fishwort, laksa leaves, mint and sweet basil

Prawns (shrimps) 500 g (1 lb 1 1/2 oz), cooked, peeled and deveined (see technique, page 207), cut in half lengthwise

Garlic chives or chives 1 bunch

Dipping sauce

Sticky rice dipping sauce (page 43) as needed

1. Dip a sheet of rice paper wrapper into warm water to soften it. Lift it up straight away. Do not allow to soak as paper will soften too much and tear easily when rolled.
2. Place rice paper on a clean, moist tea towel on a flat surface. On bottom third of rice paper, place a lettuce leaf, arrange vermicelli over lettuce and top with cucumber, bean sprouts and aromatic herbs.
3. Roll up rice paper tightly around filling (see technique, page 205). Fold in opposite sides towards the centre and over the filling. After rolling halfway, place 3–4 prawns, skin side against rice paper, tuck in garlic chive along crease, then continue rolling. Press to seal. The roll should be about 10-cm (4-in) long.
4. Repeat steps above with remaining rice paper and filling.
5. Serve with dipping sauce.

NOTE

- Substitute fresh rice vermicelli with dried rice vermicelli or *somen* noodles. For cooking instructions, see Glossary (Noodles), page 191.
- Summer rolls and dipping sauce can be made 2–3 hours ahead and chilled. Cover rolls with damp kitchen towels, then wrap in cling film.

Tomato Relish Chruok Banlè Angkâr Lign

Bean sprouts and cucumber give crunchiness, tomatoes colour and roasted ground rice texture to this relish. Serve with grilled or smoked fish.

Preparation: Short • Serves 4 to 6

Garlic 2 cloves, peeled

Galangal 1 small thumb-size knob, peeled and sliced

Small cucumber 1, sliced into fine strips

Bean sprouts 100 g (3½ oz), tailed

Nearly ripe tomatoes 4, sliced into thin strips

Shallots 2, peeled and sliced thinly

Roasted ground rice (page 33) 3 Tbsp

Salt 1 tsp

1. Place garlic and galangal in a mortar and pound until fine.
2. Combine pounded ingredients with remaining ingredients in a mixing bowl. Stand for a few hours before serving.

Vegetarian Fried Spring Rolls Nom Chienn Banlè

This recipe is the vegetarian version of the spring rolls recipe (page 48). Full of vegetables, these spring rolls offers a healthier alternative. To differentiate vegetarian spring rolls from the ones with meat, roll them in different lengths. Longer for spring rolls with meat, shorter for spring rolls with vegetables. This is particularly useful at parties when you have vegetarian guests. Served with pickled vegetables (page 46), vegetarian spring rolls make a great party food.

Preparation: Long • Cooking: 15 minutes • Serves 4 to 6

Rice paper (spring roll) wrappers 1 package, 15-cm (6-in) rounds or brick pastry sheets (*feuilles de brick*) 1 package, small, square sheets, thawed

Warm water to soften rice paper wrappers

Cooking oil for deep-frying 500 ml (16 fl oz / 2 cups)

Filling

Cooking oil 3 Tbsp

Garlic 1 tsp, peeled and chopped

Green cabbage 1/4 head, shredded

Courgette (zucchini) 1, peeled and grated

Carrot 1, peeled, grated and excess water squeezed out using your palms

Celery stalks 2, finely chopped

Small onion 1, peeled and chopped

Salt 2 pinches

Mint 1 Tbsp, chopped

1. Heat oil in a large wok over medium heat. Brown garlic. Add vegetables and stir-fry quickly for 5 minutes over high heat, until softened. Gently toss to mix well. Season with salt and sprinkle with mint. Remove from heat and allow filling to cool.
2. To make spring rolls, dip a sheet of rice paper in a shallow dish of warm water. Lift it up straight away and place on a clean moist tea towel on a flat surface. Do not leave rice paper to soak as it will tear easily when rolled. Skip this step if using brick pastry sheets.
3. On the bottom third of rice paper/pastry sheet, spread 2 Tbsp filling. Fold rice paper/pastry sheet over filling and roll up tightly. Fold in opposite ends towards the centre and over the filling, then continue rolling (see technique, page 204).
4. Repeat steps 2 and 3 until filling is used up.
5. Deep-fry over medium heat, until golden brown and crisp. Remove and drain on kitchen paper.

NOTE

- To secure a better seal, make a paste for sealing the rolls. In small saucepan, stir 1 tsp of flour with 4 Tbsp water over medium heat, until thickened. Allow to cool then brush with a little paste the final edge of rice paper to seal the roll.
- Spring rolls take a long time to prepare so make a larger quantity, if desired. Freeze uncooked spring rolls. Before deep-frying them, no thawing is necessary.

Soups

Chicken and Aubergine Coconut Milk Soup Samlar K'tis Moan Trâb

Preparation: Average • Cooking: 30 minutes • Serves 4 to 6

Coconut cream 200 ml (7 fl oz), set aside 3 Tbsp for topping

Palm sugar 1/2 tsp

Coarse salt 1 tsp

Fish sauce 2 Tbsp

Prawn (shrimp) paste 1/2 tsp

***K'tis kroeung* (page 40)** 3 Tbsp

Whole free range (organic) chicken 1.5 kg (3 lb 4 1/2 oz), boned and cut into chunks

Coconut milk 200 ml (7 fl oz)

Water 750 ml (24 fl oz / 3 cups)

Asian round aubergines (eggplants/brinjals) 10, halved

Long beans or French beans 5, cut into 4-cm (1 1/2-in) lengths

Sweet basil a handful, for garnish

1. In a pot, bring coconut cream to the boil over medium heat. Season with palm sugar, coarse salt, fish sauce, prawn paste and *k'tis kroeung*. Reduce heat to low and leave to simmer for 10 minutes, stirring occasionally.
2. Add chicken and leave to cook for another 10 minutes.
3. Gradually add coconut milk, water, aubergines and beans. Adjust seasoning and cook for a few more minutes until chicken is tender. Remove from heat.
4. Ladle into a large serving bowl, top with reserved coconut cream and garnish with sweet basil. Serve hot.

Variation

- Try this recipe with fresh bamboo shoots or pork spare ribs, cut into 3-cm (1 1/4-in) lengths.

Beef and Water Spinach Sour Soup Samlar M'chou Kroeung Sach Kô

Preparation: Average • Cooking: 30 minutes • Serves 4 to 6

Water spinach 1 bunch

Beef loin 700 g (1 1/2 lb), sliced very thinly

Yellow *kroeung* (page 39) 2 Tbsp

Salt 2 tsp

Fish sauce 2 Tbsp

***Prahok* without bones** 1 tsp, dissolved in some hot water

Wood apple (or tamarind powder) halved, 5 Tbsp scooped out from centre part

Palm sugar 1/2 tsp

Cooking oil 2 Tbsp

Water 1.5 litres (48 fl oz / 6 cups)

Kaffir lime leaves 3

Curry leaves (*kantrok*) a few leaves, for garnish

1. Wash water spinach and cut into 4-cm (1 1/2-in) sections. To prevent water spinach from turning brown, leave to soak in cold water. Drain before using.
2. In a mixing bowl, combine beef and *kroeung*. Season with salt, fish sauce, *prahok*, wood apple and palm sugar. Combine well the mixture.
3. Heat oil in a large pot over medium heat. Stir-fry mixture for about 10 minutes. Add water, then water spinach. Leave to simmer over medium heat until beef is tender. When cooking is almost done, add kaffir lime leaves.
4. Remove from heat. Ladle into a large serving bowl, garnish with curry leaves and serve immediately.

Pumpkin Soup Samlar Samlak L'peuv

Preparation: Average • Cooking: 25 minutes • Serves 4 to 6

Water 1 litre (32 fl oz / 4 cups)

Lemongrass leaves 1 bunch, rubbed lightly using your hands

Prahok 1 tsp, dissolved in a little hot water

Salt 1 tsp

Fish sauce 1 Tbsp

Pumpkin 1/2, medium, peeled and cut into small chunks

Pumpkin tendrils 3, peeled and cut into 4-cm (1 1/2-in) sections

Garlic 2 cloves, peeled and crushed

Fingerroot (Chinese keys) 4, peeled and pounded with garlic

Snakehead murrel 3 steaks

Smoked fish 2, dry-roasted to revive flavour and texture, skinned, boned, then coarsely broken

Pumpkin flowers and leaves a handful

Fresh bird's eye chilli leaves a handful

1. In a pot, bring water to the boil, add lemongrass leaves and *prahok*. Season with salt and fish sauce. Add pumpkin chunks and tendrils, garlic and fingerroot.
2. Return mixture to the boil. When pumpkin is tender, add fish steaks and smoked fish, pumpkin flowers and leaves and chilli leaves. Adjust seasoning and remove from heat.
3. Ladle into a large serving bowl and serve hot.

Variation

- Snakehead murrel (*trey ras*) is a kind of freshwater fish available in Asian stores. Substitute with mullet or tilapia.

Instant Beef Broth Samlar Chruok Krav Chhnaing Sach Kô

Preparation: Average • Serves 4 to 6

Beef loin 500 g (1 lb 1 1/2 oz), sliced thinly

White mushrooms 6, washed and sliced

Ginger 1 thumb-size knob, peeled and julienned

Lemongrass stalk 1

Shallot 1, peeled and sliced

Salt 1 tsp

Fish sauce 1 Tbsp

Lemon juice 6 Tbsp

Chicken stock (page 34) 1litre (32 fl oz / 4 cups)

Fresh aromatic herbs an assorted bunch of coriander (cilantro) leaves, chives, sawtooth coriander and sweet basil

1. Place all ingredients in a large serving bowl, except for stock and aromatic herbs.
2. Just before serving, bring chicken stock to the boil and ladle over ingredients. Add coarsely chopped aromatic herbs. Adjust seasoning. Serve immediately.

Samlar Kâko Soup Samlar Kâko

Samlar kâko is a quintessential Cambodian dish. The soup uses a wide range of fruit and vegetables, aromatic fresh leaves as well as distinctive ingredients such as *kroeung* (herb and spice paste) and *prahok* (fermented fish). It reflects the abundance, variety and unique flavours found in Cambodia.

Many versions of this soup are possible, depending on personal taste and which vegetables are in season. Try preparing with carrots, courgettes (zucchinis) or chayote.

Preparation: Long • Cooking: 30 minutes • Serves 4 to 6

Cooking oil 2 Tbsp

Green *kroeung* (page 39) 2 Tbsp, set aside 1 tsp for when cooking is almost done

Boneless pork neck 200 g (7 oz), sliced

Prahok 1 tsp, dissolved in some hot water

Salt 2 tsp

Palm sugar 1/2 tsp

Fish sauce 2 Tbsp

Roasted ground rice (page 33) 2 tsp, set aside 1 tsp for when cooking is almost done

Walking catfish 500 g (1 lb 1 1/2 oz), gutted, scaled and cut into steaks

Water 1.5 litres (48 fl oz / 6 cups)

Young bitter gourd leaves 3 stems

Fruit and Vegetables

Pumpkin 1 small slice, peeled, seeded and cubed

Green papaya 1, peeled, seeded and sliced into thin strips

Green banana 1, peeled, seeded and sliced into thin strips

Asian long aubergine (eggplant/brinjal) 1, cubed

Asian round aubergines (eggplants/brinjals) 4, halved

Pea aubergines (eggplants/brinjals) a handful

Long beans or French beans 4, cut into 4-cm (1 1/2-in) lengths

Winged beans 2, cut into 4-cm (1 1/2-in) lengths

1. Prepare fruit and vegetables.
2. In a large pot, heat oil over medium heat. Add *kroeung* and stir-fry for a few minutes until fragrant. Add pork, *prahok*, salt, palm sugar and fish sauce. Toss ingredients to coat pork evenly.
3. Cook over low heat, then add fruit and vegetables. Sprinkle with half of roasted ground rice.
4. When fruit and vegetables are nearly cooked, add fish. Pour in water and bring to the boil. Reduce heat and simmer gently, stirring carefully, to prevent fish from breaking apart. Adjust seasoning.
5. When fish is almost done, add reserved green *kroeung*, roasted ground rice and bitter gourd leaves. Remove soup from heat once fish is just cooked through.
6. Ladle into a large serving bowl and serve with steamed rice.

Variation

- Walking catfish (*trey andeng*) is a kind of freshwater fish. Alternatively, replace with two chicken breasts or quails.
- In Cambodia, bitter gourd leaves can be substituted with curry leaves (*kantrok*), *moringa oleifera* (*m'rom*) and *sesbania grandiflora* (*pkar angkear dei*).

Banana Trunk Soup

Samlar Doeum Chek

In the Cambodian countryside, banana trunks are used as pig feed. It is not an ingredient that city folks would consider eating. I discovered this soup when, as a city girl aged 20, I did my adult education training in poor rural villages. This soup is always associated in my memory with the generosity and hospitality of the village people, who invited me each time to share their meal, despite their very modest means.

Preparation: Average • Cooking: 25 minutes • Serves 4 to 6

Tender core of banana trunk 1

Water 1 litre (32 fl oz / 4 cups)

Prahok 1 tsp, dissolved in some hot water

Fresh tamarind pods 2–3, depending on size of pods

Salt 1 tsp

Fish sauce 1 Tbsp

Galangal 1 thumb-size knob, peeled

Garlic 2 cloves, peeled and pounded with galangal

Snakehead murrel 400 g (14 1/3 oz), gutted, scaled and cut into steaks

Small freshwater prawns (shrimps) a handful, head tips cut off

Holy basil a handful

1. Cut tender core of banana trunk crosswise into 4-cm (1 1/2-in) thick sections. Halve each section lengthwise, then cut into 4-cm (1 1/2-in) matchsticks.
2. In a large pot, bring water to the boil. Add *prahok*, banana trunk, tamarind pods, salt, fish sauce, galangal and garlic. Cook over medium heat until banana trunk is tender.
3. Remove tamarind pods to a large bowl. Mash with a fork, pressing against solids (pods, fibres and seeds) to extract as much juice as possible. Dilute with a ladle of hot soup stock. Strain juice. Use extracted juice to season soup.
4. Reduce heat, add fish and prawns, then simmer gently until prawns turn pink. Adjust seasoning. Garnish with holy basil just before removing from heat.
5. Ladle into a large serving bowl and serve immediately.

Variation

- Substitute fresh tamarind pods with tamarind pulp or powder, or use lime juice.
- Snakehead murrel (*trey ras*) is a kind of freshwater fish available in Asian stores. Giant snakehead (*trey chhdor*), another sort of snakehead, and *spot pangasius* (*trey po*), a sort of catfish, can also be used in this recipe. Alternatively, substitute with mackerel or tilapia.

Coconut Milk Sour Soup with Pineapple and Fishballs

Samlar M'chou K'tis Prahet Trey M'nôas

This is one of my mother's favourite soups. It blends contrasting tastes: the sweetness of the pineapple with the sourness of the tamarind. In addition, it combines different textures: firm fishballs to smooth coconut milk.

Preparation: Long • Cooking: 30 minutes • Serves 4 to 6

Fish fillets 300 g (11 oz), skinned and boned

Coconut cream 200 ml (7 fl oz), set aside 3 Tbsp for topping

***K'tis kroeung* (page 40)** 3 Tbsp

Palm sugar $^{1}/_{2}$ tsp

Prawn (shrimp) paste $^{1}/_{2}$ tsp

Coarse salt 1 tsp

Fish sauce 2 Tbsp

Small pineapple 1, peeled, cored, and cut into strips (see technique, page 211)

Tamarind juice made by mixing 20 g ($^{2}/_{3}$ oz) tamarind pulp with 200 ml (7 fl oz) hot water and strained (page 35)

Smoked fish 2, dry-roasted to revive flavour and texture, then skinned, boned and coarsely broken

Coconut milk 200 ml (7 fl oz)

Water 750 ml (24 fl oz / 3 cups)

Sweet basil a handful, for garnish

1. Pound fish in a mortar or mince in a food processor until texture is firm and smooth. Set aside.
2. In a pot, bring coconut cream to the boil over medium heat. Add *k'tis kroeung*, palm sugar, prawn paste, coarse salt and fish sauce. Reduce heat to low and leave to simmer for 10 minutes, stirring occasionally.
3. Add pineapple, tamarind juice and smoked fish. Leave to cook for another 10 minutes. Gradually pour in coconut milk, followed by water.
4. Wet hands and shape pounded or minced fish into small balls. Drop balls one by one into the soup as they are formed. Adjust seasoning. When fishballs float to the surface, remove from heat to a large serving bowl.
5. Ladle soup into a serving bowl over fishballs. Top with reserved coconut cream and garnish with sweet basil. Serve immediately.

NOTE

- In Cambodia, clown and bronze featherback (*trey kray* and *trey slat*), two varieties of featherback fish, are typically used in this dish. Alternatively, substitute with any firm white-fleshed fish.
- Fishballs bought in supermarkets are no match for homemade ones, which are healthier and tastier.
- For this recipe, choose a slightly sour pineapple. Adjust tamarind juice seasoning accordingly.

Young Stems of Lotus Sour Soup Samlar M'chou Krâ Av Chhouk

In this soup, the lotus stems provide a crunchy texture and the tamarind lends its sourness. The pineapple and tomatoes give vibrant colours to the dish. Lotus stems, not as well-known as lotus flowers, always remind me of a typical scene in Cambodia where children laugh with joy as they dive into ponds to bring back lotus stems to their mothers.

Preparation: Average • Cooking: 20 minutes • Serves 4 to 6

Chicken stock (page 34) or water 1 litre (32 fl oz / 4 cups)

Coarse salt 1 tsp

Galangal 1 small slice, peeled and crushed

Fresh pineapple 1/2, peeled, halved lengthwise, cored, then sliced

Young lotus stems 3, cut into 4-cm (1 1/2-in) lengths; fibres removed (see technique, page 206)

Nearly ripe tomatoes 2, quartered

Palm sugar 1/2 tsp

Tamarind juice made by mixing 20 g (2/3 oz) tamarind pulp with 200 ml (7 fl oz) hot water and strained (page 35)

Lemongrass stalks 2, ends trimmed, bruised

Fish sauce 2 Tbsp

Snakehead murrel 500 g (1 lb 1 1/2 oz), gutted, scaled and cut into steaks

Fresh aromatic herbs an assorted bunch of sweet basil, sawtooth coriander and rice paddy herb, coarsely chopped

Fried chopped garlic (page 34) 1 Tbsp

1. In a pot, bring chicken stock to the boil over medium heat. Add coarse salt, galangal, pineapple and lotus stems. Return stock to the boil.
2. When stock is boiling, stir in tomatoes, palm sugar, tamarind juice, lemongrass, fish sauce and fish. Return to the boil again, then reduce heat and leave to simmer for another 2 minutes. Adjust seasoning. Remove from heat.
3. Ladle into a large serving bowl, garnish with fresh aromatic herbs and sprinkle with fried garlic. Serve immediately with sliced chillies in fish sauce on the side.

Variation

- Substitute fresh pineapple with canned slices. Take 5 slices and cut each one into 8 pieces.
- Snakehead murrel (*trey ras*) is a kind of freshwater fish available in Asian stores. Alternatively, substitute with mackerel or tilapia.

Sour Prawn Soup *Sgnor Chruok Bangkang*

Sgnor is a type of Cambodian soup with a clear broth that brings out the flavour of the ingredients. It is simple and quick to prepare. In this soup, lemongrass and aromatic herbs pair well with the mild and sweet taste of freshwater prawns. For additional flavour and texture, try this recipe with a mix of saltwater prawns, mussels and squid (see photo).

Preparation: Short • Cooking: 15 minutes • Serves 4 to 6

Chicken stock (page 34) 1 litre (32 fl oz / 4 cups)

Lemongrass stalk 1, ends trimmed, halved crosswise and bruised

Kaffir lime leaves 3

Garlic 3 cloves, peeled and crushed

Salt 1 tsp

Sugar a pinch

Fish sauce 2 Tbsp

Giant freshwater prawns (shrimps) 6, deveined, shells left intact, legs trimmed (see technique, page 207)

Lime juice 3 Tbsp

Fresh aromatic herbs an assorted bunch of coriander (cilantro) leaves, chives, sawtooth coriander and sweet basil

Fried chopped garlic (page 34) 1 Tbsp

1. In a pot, bring chicken stock to the boil over medium heat. Add lemongrass, kaffir lime leaves and garlic. Season with salt, sugar and fish sauce. Leave to cook for a few minutes until aroma is released. Reduce heat and add prawns. When prawns turn pink, scoop them out and remove broth from heat.
2. Peel prawns and leave them whole or shred coarsely.
3. Place prawns in a serving bowl and ladle broth over. Season with lime juice and garnish with aromatic herbs and fried garlic. Serve immediately with sliced chillies in fish sauce on the side.

Chicken Congee Babar Moan

It is a great honour for city folks to be invited by village people to share a chicken rice congee. This is a simple dish, but it uses good quality ingredients: grain-fed free range chickens and aromatic herbs, fresh from the garden. Above all, it is a dish that is always offered in a spirit of generous and convivial hospitality.

Preparation: Average • Cooking: 30 minutes • Serves 4 to 6

Whole free range (organic) chicken 1, small (about 1.3 kg / 2 lb 14 oz), giblets optional, cut into 4 pieces

Water 2 litres (64 fl oz / 8 cups)

Long grain fragrant (jasmine) rice a handful, rinsed and drained

Salt 2 tsp

Fish sauce 2 Tbsp

Round lettuce 1 head, rinsed, pat- or spun-dry, then cut into long thin strips (chiffonade)

Bean sprouts 200 g (7 oz), tailed

Fresh green peppercorns or ground pepper to taste

Fresh aromatic herbs an assorted bunch of coriander (cilantro) leaves, chives and sawtooth coriander

Fried chopped garlic (page 34) 1 Tbsp

1. In a large pot, place chicken, chicken heart and gizzard, if using. Cover with water and cook over medium heat for 10 minutes, skimming off any impurities that rise to the surface. Add rice and salt. Reduce heat to medium-low and leave to cook for 20 minutes or until rice is tender.
2. When cooking is almost over, add chicken liver and fish sauce. Remove from heat. Shred chicken meat coarsely.
3. Place lettuce leaves, then bean sprouts at the bottom of individual serving bowls. Ladle congee into bowls and top with shredded chicken. Season with pepper and garnish with fresh aromatic herbs and fried garlic. Serve immediately.

Fish and Tamarind Leaf Soup Samlar Trey Trouy Ampil

Preparation: Average • Cooking: 30 minutes • Serves 4 to 6

Water spinach 1 bunch

Water 1.5 litres (48 fl oz / 6 cups)

Coarse salt 2 tsp

Garlic 2 cloves, peeled and crushed

Galangal 1 small slice, peeled and crushed

Fish sauce 2 Tbsp

Palm sugar 1/2 tsp

Snakehead murrel 4 steaks

Young tamarind leaves a handful

Rice paddy herb 1 Tbsp

1. Wash spinach and cut into 4-cm (1 1/2-in) sections. To prevent spinach from turning brown, leave to soak in cold water. Drain before using.
2. In a large pot, bring water to the boil. Add salt, garlic, galangal, fish sauce, palm sugar and spinach. Reduce heat and cook over medium heat until spinach is tender.
3. Add fish and tamarind leaves. Simmer over low heat until fish is just cooked through. Remove from heat.
4. Ladle into a large serving bowl and garnish with rice paddy herb.

Variation

- Snakehead murrel (*trey ras*) is a kind of freshwater fish available in Asian stores. Replace with giant snakehead (*trey chhdor*), mackerel or tilapia.
- Substitute young tamarind leaves with sorrel or 3 tsp tamarind powder.

Fish & Seafood

Steamed Salted Fish with Pork *Trey Prama Chamhoy*

Preparation: Short • Cooking: 20 minutes • Serves 4 to 6

Dried salted fish 200 g (7 oz), soaked to remove salt, skinned and boned

Minced pork 450 g (1 lb)

Eggs 3, beaten

Garlic 4 cloves, peeled and chopped

Onions 2, peeled and sliced thinly

Shallots 3, peeled and sliced

Coriander (cilantro) leaves 1 Tbsp

Fresh chives a handful, snipped

Palm sugar 1 tsp

Ground white pepper to taste

1. Chop salted fish with minced pork.
2. In a mixing bowl, combine pork mixture and all remaining ingredients. Mix well to ensure a smooth consistency.
3. Transfer mixture to a shallow heatproof bowl and steam for 20 minutes until cooked. Alternatively, fry in a pan to make an omelette.
4. Serve with steamed rice and crunchy vegetables such as cabbage, aubergines (eggplants/brinjals), young ginger root, cucumber and long beans.

Stir-fried Salmon with Vegetables *Trey Chienn T'cha Banlè*

Preparation: Short • Marinating: 15 minutes • Cooking: 15 minutes • Serves 4 to 6

Salmon or cod fillets 600 g (1 lb 5 1/3 oz), skinned and boned, sliced thinly

Lime juice 3 Tbsp

Olive oil 2 Tbsp

Asparagus spears 300 g (11 oz), bottom part of spears peeled, cut in half crosswise, then blanched

Red and yellow capsicums (bell peppers) 1 each, white pith and seeds removed, julienned

Baby corn 200 g (7 oz)

Carrot 1 peeled and cut into thin strips

Onion 1, peeled and quartered

Salt to taste

Crushed white pepper 2 pinches

Lime 1, sliced, for garnish

1. Place fish slices in a large shallow plate. Pour over lime juice and olive oil. Cover and leave to marinate for 15 minutes.
2. Heat oil in a large wok over medium heat. Stir-fry briefly all the vegetables until almost tender yet crunchy. Season with salt and crushed white pepper. Remove from heat and keep warm.
3. Pan-fry marinated fish slices over high heat for a few minutes or until fish is just cooked.
4. On a large serving plate, arrange stir-fried vegetables, top with fish and garnish with lime slices.

Fish Amok Amok Trey

Amok is a typical Cambodian dish. It is a combination of fish, coconut milk and *kroeung* served in banana leaf cups. Steaming enhances the flavour of the ingredients and gives amok its unique, moist texture.

Preparation: Long • Cooking: 15 minutes • Serves 4 to 6

Banana leaves to make banana leaf cups

Topping

Coconut cream 3 Tbsp

Salt 2 pinches

Corn flour (cornstarch) or plain flour 1 tsp

Fish mixture

Yellow *kroeung* (page 39) 3 Tbsp

Fingerroot (Chinese keys) 1 tsp, peeled, chopped and pounded with yellow *kroeung*

Snakehead murrel 600 g (1 lb 5 1/3 oz), skinned, boned and sliced thinly

Eggs 2, beaten

Fish sauce 2 Tbsp

Salt 1/2 tsp

Palm sugar 1/2 tsp

Coconut cream 150 ml (5 fl oz)

Garnish

Young noni leaves a handful

Red capsicum (bell pepper) 1, white pith and seeds removed, julienned

Kaffir lime leaves 3, centre vein removed and cut into fine strips

1. Start by making make small banana leaf cups about 12-cm (5-in) in diameter (see technique, page 217).
2. Prepare topping. In a small pan, combine 3 Tbsp coconut cream, salt and corn flour. Bring to the boil, stirring constantly until coconut cream thickens. Remove from heat and set aside.
3. Prepare fish mixture. In a large bowl, combine yellow *kroeung*, fingerroot, fish, beaten eggs and fish sauce. Mix well. Season with salt and palm sugar. Add coconut cream. Stir vigorously until smooth, using a wooden spatula.
4. Before steaming fish mixture, check seasoning by cooking a small quantity in a pan or microwave oven. Adjust seasoning to taste.
5. For each cup, arrange noni leaves at the bottom, then add fish mixture, using a spoon to level and flatten. Add topping and garnish with capsicum strips and kaffir lime leaves. Steam for 5–8 minutes or until *amok* is cooked through, with a firm and moist texture.
6. Remove from steamer and serve immediately with rice.

Variation

- Banana leaves are available in most Asian stores. Alternatively, use individual ramekins or heatproof bowls. With the banana leaves, you can also make larger 20–25-cm (8–10-in) diameter cups. Larger cups will require another 10 minutes in the steamer.
- If snakehead murrel (*trey ras*) is not available, substitute with any firm white-fleshed fish fillets such as cod or try using chicken breast fillets, prawns or scallops. Chicken will require another 5–10 minutes in the steamer.
- Substitute noni leaves with spinach leaves or shredded cabbage for a crunchier texture.

Pan-fried Sea Bream with Green Mango Trey Chienn Svay Kchey

Preparation: Short • Cooking: 15 minutes • Serves 4 to 6

Sea bream 600 g (1 lb 5¹/₃ oz), gutted and scaled

Cooking oil 2 Tbsp

Green mangoes 1–2, depending on size, peeled and finely sliced into strips

Shallots 2, peeled and finely sliced

Fish sauce 1 Tbsp

Fresh bird's eye chillies (optional) 2, seeded and thinly sliced

1. Using a sharp knife, score fish with two diagonal cuts on each side.
2. Heat oil in a wok over high heat. Pan-fry sea bream until crisp and golden brown on one side, then turn fish over to cook the other side. Remove and drain on kitchen paper.
3. Arrange fish on a serving dish, garnish with green mango strips and top with shallots. Drizzle with fish sauce mixed with sliced chillies. Serve immediately with steamed rice.

Variation

- Sea bream can be substituted with tilapia or salmon steaks.

Charcoal-grilled Fish with Tamarind Dipping Sauce

Trey Dot Teuk Trey Ampil Tom

This light and aromatic meal is easy to prepare. Grill over charcoal or in a banana trunk (see technique, page 214). Alternatively, cook on a barbecue or under a conventional grill.

Preparation: Short • Cooking: 30 minutes • Serves 4 to 6

Snakehead murrel 1.2 kg (2 lb 11 oz), gutted and scaled

Neem, young leaves and flowers 2 bunches, blanched

Round lettuce 1 head, rinsed, pat- or spun-dry

Cucumber 1, halved lengthwise, then sliced

Bean sprouts 2 handfuls, tailed

Fresh aromatic herbs an assorted bunch of mint, fishwort, laksa leaves and sweet basil

Tamarind dipping sauce (page 45) 250 ml (8 fl oz / 1 cup)

1. Using a sharp knife, score fish with several diagonal cuts on each side.
2. Grill fish until cooked through.
3. Transfer fish to a serving dish. Arrange neem leaves and flowers, lettuce, cucumber, bean sprouts and assorted herbs on a large serving plate. Pour tamarind sauce into individual dipping bowls.
4. Allow guests to assemble the dish for themselves. Place a piece of fish on a lettuce leaf, top with cucumber and bean sprouts, then garnish with neem leaves and flowers and plenty of aromatic herbs. Roll up the lettuce leaf and dip into tamarind dipping sauce before eating.

Variation

- Snakehead murrel (*trey ras*) is a kind of freshwater fish available in some Asian stores. Giant snakehead (*trey chhdor*) and walking catfish (*trey andeng*) can also be used in this recipe. Alternatively, substitute with salmon or mullet.
- Tamarind dipping sauce can also be replaced with peanut and galangal sauce (page 44).

Baked Salmon in Banana Leaves

Trey Kab

Cooking in *papillote* (wrapped in a parcel) brings out all the flavours of the fish and the banana leaves in which it is wrapped. The fish also remains moist as it cooks in its own juice. The banana leaves provide a beautiful presentation to this dish.

Preparation: Short • Marinating: 10 minutes • Cooking: 30 minutes • Serves 4 to 6

Cooking oil 4 Tbsp

Yellow *kroeung* (page 39) 6 Tbsp

Onions 2, peeled and sliced thinly

Red and yellow capsicums (bell peppers) 1/2 each, white pith and seeds removed, julienned

Salt to taste

Fish sauce 2 Tbsp

Lemon juice 3 Tbsp

Salmon steaks or any firm, thick fleshed-fish 6 steaks

Banana leaves for wrapping, wiped with a clean, moist tea towel

Sweet basil 1 bunch

Kaffir lime leaves 5, centre vein removed and cut into fine strips

Lemon 1, sliced thinly

Fresh bird's eye chilli (optional) 1

Toothpicks for securing banana leaf parcels

1. Preheat oven to 220°C (425°F).
2. Heat oil in a wok over medium heat. Add yellow *kroeung*, onions and capsicums. Season with salt and fish sauce. Stir well until aroma is released. Remove from heat and allow to cool, then add lemon juice.
3. Place fish steaks in this mixture for about 10 minutes.
4. Remove tough centre vein from banana leaves, then cut leaves into 12 large squares.
5. To make a parcel, first stack two banana leaf squares together. This will hold better the fish preparation. Place a fish steak with *kroeung* mixture in the centre. Make sure mixture is evenly spread over fish. Garnish with sweet basil, kaffir lime leaves and slices of lemon. Top with chilli, if using.
6. Fold two opposite sides of leaf over fish preparation. Close open ends and secure with toothpicks. Repeat to make another 5 parcels.
7. Place banana leaf parcels on an oven tray. Bake for about 10 minutes in a moderately hot oven (200°C / 400°F) or until fish is cooked through.
8. Unwrap parcels just before serving.

Charcoal-grilled Prawns Bangkang Aing

Preparation: Short • Cooking: 10 minutes • Serves 4 to 6

Cooking oil 2 Tbsp, or as needed

Fresh chives 2 Tbsp, snipped

Giant freshwater prawns 12, deveined, shells left intact (see technique, page 207)

Round lettuce 1 head, rinsed, pat- or spun-dry

Cucumber 1, halved lengthwise, then sliced

Fresh rice vermicelli 1 kg (2 lb 3 oz)

Fresh aromatic herbs an assorted bunch of fishwort, laksa leaves, mint and sweet basil

Lime juice sauce (page 43) 250 ml (8 fl oz / 1 cup)

1. Heat oil in a saucepan over medium heat. Remove from heat and add chives. Set aside.
2. Place prawns on charcoal, barbecue or grill and cook on each side. From time to time, brush with chive oil. Keep the cooking time short to ensure that prawns remain moist. Grill in batches to monitor cooking time.
3. When prawns turn pink, remove from heat and shell them. Place prawns on a serving plate and drizzle with remaining chive oil. Arrange vegetables, rice vermicelli and assorted herbs on a large serving plate. Transfer lime juice sauce into individual dipping bowls.
4. To serve, place a prawn on a lettuce leaf, add a slice of cucumber, some rice vermicelli and plenty of aromatic herbs. Roll up leaf and dip into lime juice sauce.

Variation

- Substitute fresh rice vermicelli with dried rice vermicelli or *somen* noodles. For cooking instructions, see Glossary (Noodles), page 191.

Steamed Silver Pomfret *Trey Chap Chamhoy*

Preparation: Short • Cooking: 15 minutes • Serves 4 to 6

Silver pomfret 1 whole, about 700 g (1 1/2 lb), gutted and scaled

Ginger 1 thumb-size knob, peeled and julienned

Shallots 2, peeled and sliced

Spring onions (scallions) 2, sliced

Salted soy beans 2 Tbsp, drained

Light soy sauce 1 Tbsp

Sesame oil 1 Tbsp

Vegetable stock (page 35) or water 2 Tbsp

Garnish

Fresh chives 2 Tbsp, cut into 2-cm (3/4-in) lengths

Coriander (cilantro) leaves 1 small bunch

Red capsicum (bell pepper) 1, white pith and seeds removed, julienned, for garnish

1. Using a sharp knife, score fish with two diagonal cuts on each side.
2. Transfer fish to a shallow heatproof plate. Top with ginger, shallots, spring onions and salted soy beans. Season with soy sauce and sesame oil. Pour a little vegetable stock or water over fish.
3. Steam for 10–15 minutes or until fish is just cooked.
4. Using a spatula, carefully transfer fish together with steaming juices onto a serving plate. Garnish with fresh chives, coriander leaves and capsicum strips. Serve immediately with steamed rice.

Variation

- Silver pomfret can be substituted with any firm white-fleshed fish.

Caramel Fish Trey Khar

Preparation: Short • Marinating: 10 minutes • Cooking: 30 minutes • Serves 4 to 6

Garlic 4 cloves, peeled

Ginger 1 thumb-size knob, peeled and chopped

Coarse salt 1 tsp

White peppercorns to taste

Dark soy sauce 1 Tbsp

Fish sauce 1 Tbsp

Snakehead murrel steaks 6

Palm sugar or brown sugar 1 Tbsp

Water 750 ml (24 fl oz / 3 cups)

1. Pound garlic, ginger, salt and peppercorns in a mortar. Mix in soy and fish sauces. Transfer to a shallow, non-metallic plate and leave fish to marinate in the mixture for 10 minutes.
2. Prepare caramel sauce. Put palm sugar in a heavy-based saucepan with a little water. Bring to the boil over low heat, stirring occasionally until sugar has completely dissolved. When sugar begins to colour, gently swirl pan until sugar is a deep golden brown. Remove from heat. Add fish and marinade juices to caramel sauce.
3. Bring mixture to the boil over medium heat. When it starts to bubble, add remaining water and simmer for 20 minutes over low heat until fish is cooked through.
4. Serve hot with steamed rice, shredded green mango and cucumber slices.

Variation

- Snakehead murrel (*trey ras*) can be substituted with whole mackerels (*trey plathou*) or *trey linh* (*Thynnichthys thynnoides*).

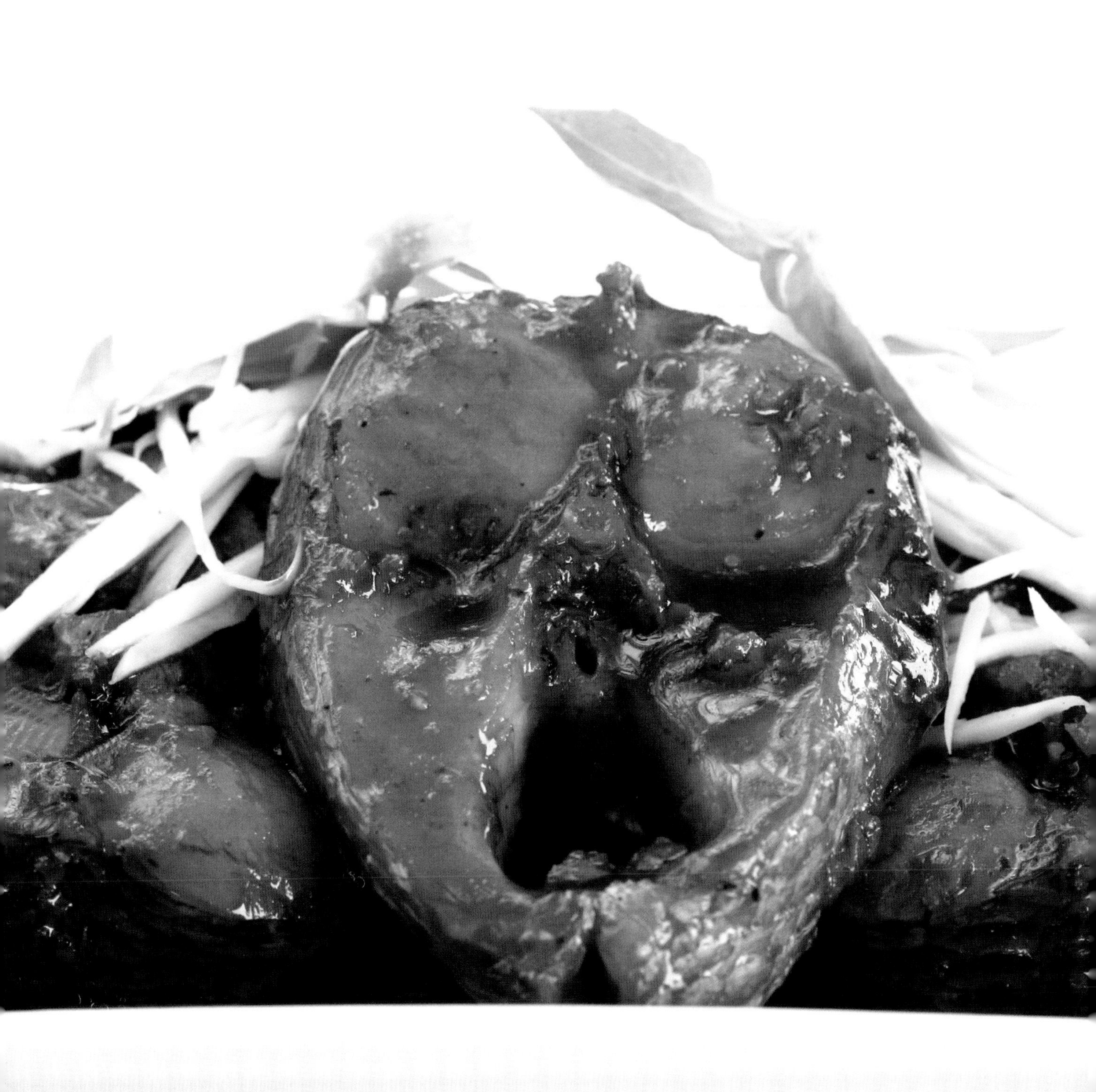

Fried Fish with Salted Soy Beans Trey Chienn Sieng

In Cambodia, two varieties of catfish, *trey taon* and *trey kes*, are used when preparing this dish.

Preparation: Average • Cooking: 20 minutes • Serves 4 to 6

Firm-fleshed fish (sea bream or tilapia) 1 whole, about 600 g (1 lb 5¹/₃ oz), gutted and scaled

Cooking oil 5 Tbsp

Ginger 1 thumb-size knob, peeled and julienned

Garlic 3 cloves, peeled and finely chopped

Shallots 2, sliced

Spring onions (scallions) 2, sliced

Salted soy beans 2 Tbsp, drained

Palm sugar 1 Tbsp

Palm vinegar or white wine vinegar 2 Tbsp

Water 100 ml (3¹/₂ fl oz)

Red capsicum (bell pepper) ¹/₂, white pith and seeds removed, julienned

Fresh chives 1 tsp, snipped

Coriander (cilantro) leaves a handful

1. Using a sharp knife, score fish with several diagonal cuts on each side.
2. Heat oil in a frying pan over medium heat. Fry fish until golden brown and crispy on both sides. Remove from heat and drain on kitchen paper. Keep warm.
3. Prepare sauce. Fry ginger and garlic over low heat until golden. Add shallots, spring onions, salted soy beans, palm sugar, palm vinegar and water. Simmer for 5 minutes over low heat.
4. Arrange fish on a serving plate. Drizzle with sauce and garnish with capsicum, chives and coriander. Serve hot with rice.

Stir-fried Crab with Kampot Green Peppercorns

T'cha K'dam Samot M'rec Kchey Kampot

This is my son's favourite recipe. The taste of the green peppercorns complements well the more subtle flavour of fresh crabs. The peppercorns from Kampot are world-renowned and used by top chefs in France.

Preparation: Average • Cooking: 10 minutes • Serves 4 to 6

Crabs 8

Cooking oil 2 Tbsp

Garlic 4 cloves, peeled and chopped

Spring onions (scallions) 1 bunch, white part sliced, green tops cut into 4-cm (1 1/2-in) lengths

Fresh Kampot green peppercorns 10 vines

Salt 2 pinches

Sugar 2 pinches

Coriander (cilantro) leaves a handful

1. Soak crabs in ice cold water for 30 minutes. This will firm up the flesh. Prepare crabs, leaving flesh in claws and legs (see technique, page 208).
2. Heat oil in a large wok over medium heat. Brown garlic and white part of spring onions. Add crabs and green peppercorns. Season with salt and sugar. Stir-fry quickly over high heat. When crabs turn bright orange, add green tops of spring onions.
3. Remove from heat, transfer to a serving plate and garnish with coriander leaves. Serve hot.

Stir-fried Mussels with Sweet Basil T'cha Krom T'chi Nieng Vong

For this recipe, use green shell mussels from New Zealand. They can be found in the frozen food section of Asian stores.

Preparation: Average • Cooking: 10 minutes • Serves 4 to 6

Green shell mussels 1 kg (2 lb 3 oz)

Plain (all-purpose) flour 1 tsp

Palm sugar 1 tsp

Tamarind juice made by mixing 20 g (2/3 oz) tamarind pulp with 200 ml (7 fl oz) hot water and strained (page 35)

Oyster sauce 1 tsp

Fish sauce 1 tsp

Cooking oil 3 Tbsp

Shallots a handful, peeled and sliced

Sweet basil 2 handfuls

Fresh long and mild red chilli (optional) 1, seeded and sliced

1. Prepare mussels. Using a kitchen brush, scrub mussels and remove beards. Clean thoroughly and drain. Discard mussels with broken or open shells.
2. Bring a large pot of water to the boil. Add mussels and cook for 1 minute, then drain.
3. Prepare tamarind sauce. In a mixing bowl, dissolve flour and palm sugar in tamarind juice. Stir in oyster and fish sauces.
4. Heat oil in a wok over medium heat. Fry shallots until golden. Add mussels and tamarind sauce. Continue cooking until sauce thickens. Stir in sweet basil and sliced chilli, if using.
5. Discard any unopened mussels and transfer to a serving plate. Serve immediately with steamed rice.

Stir-fried Prawns with Straw Mushrooms T'cha Bangkea Pset Chamboeung

Preparation: Short • Cooking: 25 minutes • Serves 4 to 6

Medium-size prawns (shrimps) 500 g (1 lb 1½ oz), peeled and deveined (see technique, page 207), leaving tails intact

Corn flour (cornstarch) 1 tsp

Cooking oil 4 Tbsp

Garlic 2 cloves, peeled and chopped

Carrot 1, peeled and sliced

Sliced bamboo shoots 1 small can, rinsed, blanched for 5 minutes and drained

Straw mushrooms 200 g (7 oz), stalks trimmed, rinsed and drained

Salt 2 pinches

Ground white pepper a pinch

Palm sugar ½ tsp

Fish sauce 2 Tbsp

Hard-boiled quail eggs 12, peeled

Red capsicum (bell pepper) ½, white pith and seeds removed, julienned

Coriander (cilantro) leaves a handful

1. In a mixing bowl, coat prawns with corn flour.
2. In a wok, heat 2 Tbsp oil over medium-high heat. Brown garlic. Add sliced carrot, bamboo shoots and straw mushrooms. Season with salt, pepper, palm sugar and fish sauce. Toss gently to mix well.
3. Stir-fry vegetables briefly over high heat. Remove from wok.
4. Add remaining oil to wok. When hot, add prawns and quail eggs and stir-fry over high heat. When prawns just turn pink, return vegetables to wok, add capsicum and cook for another minute.
5. Transfer to a serving plate and garnish with coriander leaves. Serve hot.

Grilled Fish and Prahok Dipping Sauce Teuk Kroeung

Preparation: Short • Cooking: 5 minutes • Serves 4 to 6

***Prahok* without bones** 1 Tbsp

Garlic 2 cloves, peeled and crushed

Shallots 2, peeled and sliced

Banana leaves for wrapping

Grilled or boiled snakehead murrel 400 g (14 1/3 oz), boned and broken into small pieces

Lime juice 3 Tbsp

Sweet basil 1 bunch

Fresh chives a handful

Assorted vegetables a selection of cabbage, winged beans, aubergines (eggplants/brinjals), water spinach

Bull's horn green peppers 3, roasted and sliced

1. Wrap *prahok*, garlic and shallots in banana leaves. Roast until aroma is released. Unwrap, transfer *prahok* preparation to a mixing bowl and dissolve in some water. Leave to stand for a few minutes.
2. In a mixing bowl, combine fish and *prahok* preparation and season with lime juice. Garnish with sweet basil and chives.
3. Serve with fresh crunchy vegetables such as cabbage, winged beans, aubergines and water spinach, roasted green peppers and steamed rice.

Variation

- Walking catfish (*trey andeng*), mackerel or any firm white-fleshed fish can be used in this recipe.

Smoked Fish and Aubergine Dipping Sauce Teuk Kroeung Battambang

This is a popular dish from the Battambang province where it is called *nom bok m'preuk*. In this recipe, smoked fish (*trey kes*) can be substituted with grilled fish.

Preparation: Short • Cooking: 5 minutes • Serves 4 to 6

***Prahok* without bones** 1 Tbsp

Banana leaves for wrapping

Cooking oil 1 Tbsp

Garlic 1 head, peeled

Shallots 5, peeled

Fresh bird's eye chillies 3, seeded and sliced

Pea aubergines (eggplants/brinjals) a handful

Smoked catfish 2, dry-roasted, skinned, boned and coarsely broken

Palm sugar 1 tsp

Lime juice 2 Tbsp

Water as needed

1. Wrap *prahok* in banana leaves. Roast until aroma is released.
2. Heat oil in a wok over medium heat. Fry garlic, shallots, chillies and pea aubergines. When golden brown in colour, transfer to a mortar. Add *prahok* and pound. Add smoked fish, palm sugar and lime juice. Repeat to pound into a smooth paste. Stir enough water into paste to get a thick dipping sauce.
3. Serve with steamed rice and fresh crunchy vegetables such as cucumber, green cabbage, winged beans, Asian round aubergines, water spinach, long beans and young ginger root.

Meat & Poultry

Five-spice Stuffed Duck Tear Tim

Preparation: Long • Cooking: 2 hours 30 minutes • Serves 4 to 6

Whole duck 1.5 kg (3 lb 4½ oz), cleaned inside and out

Salt 1 tsp

Crushed white pepper 1 pinch

Cooking oil 3 Tbsp

Coriander (cilantro) leaves a handful, for garnish

Stuffing

Cooking oil 1 Tbsp

Minced pork 200 g (7 oz)

Dried shiitake mushrooms 5, soaked in lukewarm water to soften for 20 minutes, drained and cut into thin strips

Lotus seeds ½ can

Garlic 3 cloves, peeled

Shallots 3, peeled

Dried banana flowers (blossoms) 1 Tbsp, soaked, rinsed and drained

Mung bean vermicelli (glass noodles) a handful, soaked in lukewarm water to soften for 10 minutes, drained and cut into 4-cm (1½-in) lengths

Whole unsalted peanuts 2 Tbsp

Palm sugar ½ tsp

Light soy sauce 1 Tbsp

Five-spice powder 1 tsp

Salt 1 tsp

Crushed white pepper 1 pinch

1. Prepare stuffing. Heat oil in a frying pan over medium heat. Add all ingredients for stuffing and fry, stirring frequently to prevent minced pork from sticking together in lumps. Remove from heat when minced pork is just cooked.
2. Rub duck cavity with salt and pepper. Heat oil in a casserole pot, add duck and cook until browned all over. Remove from heat.
3. Loosely fill duck cavity with pork stuffing. Do not pack tight as stuffing will expand during cooking. Set aside any excess stuffing for cooking in pot later. To close cavity opening, sew or use small skewers.
4. Return duck to casserole pot and cover with lukewarm water. Bring to the boil. Reduce heat and simmer for 2 hours, stirring occasionally. When cooking is almost done, arrange remaining pork stuffing around duck. When duck is cooked through and tender, remove from heat.
5. Serve garnished with coriander.

Chicken Curry Samlar Cari Moan

Preparation: Average • Cooking: 30 minutes • Serves 4 to 6

Cooking oil 3 Tbsp

Red *kroeung* (page 40) 2 Tbsp

Prawn (shrimp) paste 1 tsp

Palm sugar 1/2 tsp

Coconut cream 400 ml (13 1/3 fl oz / 1 2/3 cups)

Whole free range (organic) chicken 1.5 kg (3 lb 4 1/2 oz), with giblets, cut into chunky pieces

Coarse salt 1 tsp

Fish sauce 1 Tbsp

Coconut milk 400 ml (13 1/3 fl oz / 1 2/3 cups)

Water 250 ml (8 fl oz / 1 cup)

Long beans or French beans a handful, cut into 4-cm (1 1/2-in) lengths

Asian aubergines (eggplants/brinjals) 2, cut into chunks, soaked in cold water, then drained

Sweet potatoes 3, peeled, cut into chunks

1. Heat oil in a wok over low heat. Add red *kroeung*, prawn paste and palm sugar. Stir-fry until fragrant. Add coconut cream, chicken and giblets. Season with salt and fish sauce.
2. Stir in coconut milk and water, add long beans and aubergines. Bring to the boil, then reduce heat and simmer over medium heat until chicken is tender. Add sweet potatoes and continue cooking until curry is reduced and thick.
3. Serve with steamed rice, fresh rice vermicelli and crunchy vegetables such as cucumber or bean sprouts.

NOTE

- The curry will be tastier if you prepare this recipe using homemade coconut milk (page 36).

Stir-fried Chicken with Baby Corn T'cha Moan Sniet Pot

Preparation: Short • Cooking: 15 minutes • Serves 4 to 6

Free range (organic) chicken breast fillets 600 g (1 lb 5 1/3 oz), sliced thinly

Cooking oil 4 Tbsp

Garlic 2 cloves, peeled and chopped

Spring onions (scallions) 2, white parts quartered, green tops cut into 4-cm (1 1/2-in) lengths

Coriander (cilantro) leaves a handful, for garnish

Marinade

Oyster sauce 2 Tbsp

Fish sauce 2 tsp

Corn flour (cornstarch) 2 tsp

Salt a pinch

Ground white pepper to taste

Vegetables

Baby corn 10, blanched and rinsed in cold water

Dried black fungus 1 Tbsp, soaked in lukewarm water to soften for 20 minutes, drained, stemmed and sliced coarsely

Snow peas (mange-tout peas) a handful, trimmed

Red capsicum (bell pepper) 1/2, white pith and seeds removed, julienned

1. In a mixing bowl, combine ingredients for marinade. Add chicken breast fillets. Mix well and leave to marinate.
2. Heat 2 Tbsp oil in a wok over medium-high heat. Brown garlic and white part of spring onions, then add vegetables. Stir-fry briefly until vegetables are almost softened, yet crunchy. Remove from heat and set aside.
3. Add remaining oil to wok and heat. Add chicken and stir-fry quickly over high heat. As chicken starts to cook, return vegetables to wok and continue to stir-fry for another minute. Adjust seasoning. Remove from heat.
4. Garnish with green tops of spring onions and coriander. Serve hot with steamed rice.

Pot-roasted Chicken with Lemongrass Moan Dot Knong Chhnaing

Preparation: Short • Cooking: 40 minutes • Serves 4 to 6

Whole free range (organic) chicken 1.5 kg (3 lb 4½ oz), cleaned inside and out

Coarse salt 2 pinches

Ground white pepper to taste

Garlic 2 cloves, unpeeled and lightly crushed

Lemongrass stalks and leaves 6

Water about 100 ml (3½ fl oz)

Cooking oil 2 Tbsp

Sauce

Lime juice extracted from 2 limes

Crushed white pepper 2 pinches

Salt to taste

1. Rub chicken cavity with salt, pepper and crushed garlic, then fill cavity with 3 lemongrass stalks.
2. In a casserole pot, arrange remaining lemongrass stalks at the bottom. Pour over a little water to prevent juices from burning whilst cooking. Place chicken on top, then drizzle with oil. Cover pot with a lid and cook over medium heat for 30 minutes.
3. Halfway through cooking, turn chicken over and baste with the juices released. Continue cooking for another 10 minutes until skin is golden brown and crispy and flesh is juicy. Remove from heat.
4. Combine ingredients for sauce and transfer to a serving bowl.
5. Cut chicken in bite-size pieces and serve with sauce on the side.

Grilled Chicken with Fresh Herbs Pleuv Moan Aing

Preparation: Short • Resting: 20 minutes • Cooking: 20 minutes • Serves 4 to 6

Free range chicken thighs or breasts 6

Stuffing

Garlic 3 cloves, peeled and crushed

Shallots 2 peeled and sliced

Salt 1 tsp

White peppercorns to taste

Palm sugar 1 tsp

Fresh chives 1 Tbsp, snipped

Coriander (cilantro) leaves 2 Tbsp, chopped

Cooking oil 2 Tbsp

1. Prepare stuffing. Pound garlic, shallots, salt, white peppercorns and palm sugar in a mortar. Stir in, without pounding, chives, coriander and oil. Mix well.
2. To stuff a chicken thigh, carefully lift chicken skin using the tip of a sharp knife. Fill with stuffing using a small spoon. Leave to stand for 20 minutes.
3. Preheat oven to 220°C (425°F).
4. Arrange chicken thighs skin-side up on a roasting tin. Pour over a little water to prevent juices from burning whilst cooking. Grill for 20 minutes or until cooked and skin is golden brown and crispy. Remove from heat.
5. Place chicken thighs on a serving plate and drizzle with dripping from roasting tin. Serve immediately.

Barbecued Stuffed Chicken Wings Slab Moan Nhat Kroeung

In Cambodia, this recipe is also prepared with frogs (see photo). It is a regional delicacy from Ang Ta Som in the Takeo province.

Preparation: Short • Resting: 20 minutes • Cooking: 25 minutes • Serves 4 to 6

Green *kroeung* (page 39) 4 Tbsp

Coconut cream 200 ml (7 fl oz)

Fish sauce 1 Tbsp

Salt 2 pinches

Sugar 2 pinches

Minced meat (pork, chicken or turkey) 400 g (14 1/3 oz)

Mung bean vermicelli (glass noodles) a handful, soaked in lukewarm water to soften for 10 minutes, then drained and cut into 4-cm (1 1/2-in) lengths

Unsalted peanuts 2 Tbsp, roasted and ground

Chicken wings 20, boned

Cooking oil 3 Tbsp

1. Prepare stuffing. In a mixing bowl, dissolve green *kroeung* in coconut cream. Season with fish sauce, salt and sugar. Add minced meat, vermicelli and ground peanuts. Mix well. Leave to stand for 20 minutes.
2. To stuff a chicken wing, carefully lift chicken skin, using the tip of a sharp knife. Loosely fill with stuffing, using a small spoon. Do not pack tight as stuffing will expand during cooking. Secure with toothpicks. Repeat with remaining chicken wings.
3. Prepare barbecue. Brush chicken wings with a little oil and grill for 25 minutes, occasionally turning wings over until golden brown and crisp on each side. Alternatively, grill in an oven at 180°C (350°F) for 25–30 minutes. When cooked through, remove from heat.

NOTE

- Boned chicken wings are available from some Asian butchers. Alternatively, ask your butcher to do it for you.

Barbecued Poussins with Honey Konn Moan Aing

Preparation: Average • Marinating: 1 hour • Cooking: 30 minutes • Serves 4 to 6

Poussins (*coquelets*) 3, butterflied

Marinade

Palm vinegar or white wine vinegar 2 Tbsp

Smooth runny honey 5 Tbsp

Ginger 1 thumb-size knob, peeled and chopped

Garlic 3 cloves, peeled and crushed

Paprika powder 1 Tbsp

Salt 1 Tbsp

Crushed white pepper 2 pinches

1. Prepare marinade. Put palm vinegar and honey in a saucepan. Cook over low heat, stirring occasionally until mixture has reduced and thickened. Set aside. In a bowl, combine ginger, garlic, paprika, salt and pepper. Stir in honey mixture. Mix well.
2. Rub poussins all over with marinade. Cover and leave in the refrigerator for 1 hour.
3. Prepare barbecue. Grill poussins for 30 minutes, occasionally turning over and brushing with a little marinade until golden brown and crisp on each side. Alternatively, grill in an oven at 200°C (400°F). When cooked through, remove from heat.
4. Serve with stir-fried vegetables and steamed rice.

NOTE

- Ask your butcher to butterfly the poussins for you.

Roasted Lamb with Prahok Dipping Sauce Sach Chiem Dot Teuk Prahok

Preparation: Short • Resting: 2 hours 20 minutes • Cooking: 1 hour 30 minutes • Serves 4 to 6

Leg of lamb 1.5 kg (3 lb 4½ oz)

Garlic 4 cloves, peeled and halved

Olive oil 3 Tbsp

Water about 100 ml (3½ fl oz)

***Prahok* dipping sauce (page 45)** 1.5 litres (48 fl oz / 6 cups)

1. Wash lamb and pat dry with kitchen paper. Using the tip of a sharp knife, make small incisions all over meat. Insert garlic into incisions. Rub 2 Tbsp olive oil all over meat, then cover with cling film. Leave to stand for 2 hours at room temperature.
2. Preheat oven to 250°C (475°F). Grease a roasting tin with remaining oil. Pour over a little water to prevent juices from burning whilst cooking. Place lamb in tin. Turn down oven to 180ºC (350°F) and roast lamb, allowing 30 minutes per 500 g (1 lb 1½ oz).
3. Baste lamb occasionally with the juices released. Halfway through cooking, turn lamb over for an even roast. Squeeze with tongs to see if roasted lamb is cooked to your liking. Rare feels soft, medium rare has little resistance while well-done feels quite firm. Do not insert a skewer to test for doneness as this may cause the juices to flow out, resulting in a dry roast.
4. Remove lamb and transfer to a serving plate. Cover with foil and allow meat to rest for 15–20 minutes before carving.
5. Serve lamb with steamed rice and prahok dipping sauce on the side.

Stir-fried Beef with Eggs and Tomatoes Loc Lac

Preparation: Short • Cooking: 20 minutes • Serves 4 to 6

Round lettuce 1 head, rinsed, pat- or spun-dry

Tomatoes 3, sliced

Small onion 1, peeled and sliced

Hard-boiled eggs 3, peeled and cut into quarters

Beef fillet 600 g (1 lb $5^1/_3$ oz), diced

Corn flour (cornstarch) 1 tsp

Cooking oil 1 Tbsp

Sauce

Lemon juice 1 Tbsp

Salt 2 pinches

Ground white pepper 3 pinches

1. Combine ingredients for sauce. Set aside.
2. Arrange lettuce on a large platter. Arrange tomato, onion and hard-boiled eggs over lettuce.
3. In a mixing bowl, rub meat all over with corn flour. Heat oil in a wok over medium-high heat. Add beef cubes and stir-fry until medium rare.
4. Remove from heat and arrange stir-fried beef over vegetables. Serve immediately with sauce on the side.

Khmer Steamboat Tch'hav Han Khmer

This is a festive dish that creates a warm and friendly atmosphere around the table as everyone shares food from a central pot. For this recipe, use a steamboat (hot pot) with portable gas stove or hot coals. Alternatively, use a large fondue set over electric hot plates.

Preparation: Long • Cooking: 20 minutes • Serves 4 to 6

Beef fillet 1.2 kg (2 lb 11 oz), sliced thinly

Egg yolk 1

Fresh rice vermicelli 1 kg (2 lb 3 oz)

Round lettuce 2 heads, rinsed, pat- or spun-dry

Cucumber 1, halved lengthwise, then sliced thinly

Bean sprouts 300 g (11 oz), tailed

Fresh aromatic herbs an assorted bunch of fishwort, laksa leaves, mint and sweet basil

Broth

Galangal 5 thin slices, peeled

Garlic 5 cloves, unpeeled

Shallots 3, unpeeled

Unsalted peanuts 5 Tbsp, roasted and ground

Chicken stock (page 34) 2 litres

Fish sauce 8 Tbsp

White wine vinegar or lime juice 8 Tbsp

Sugar 4 Tbsp

NOTE

- The broth and rice vermicelli (if not using fresh vermicelli) can be prepared a day ahead.

1. Prepare broth. In a pan, dry-roast galangal, unpeeled garlic and shallots over medium heat. When aroma is released and garlic and shallots skins are black, remove from heat. Allow garlic and shallots to cool, then peel skins. Place ingredients in a mortar and pound into a smooth paste. Alternatively, use a food processor. Set paste aside. In a large mixing bowl, combine chicken stock, fish sauce, white wine vinegar and sugar. Mix well. Add paste and stir to dissolve. Set broth aside.
2. Arrange beef slices on a large serving plate, forming a well in the centre. Place egg yolk in the well. Arrange rice vermicelli, vegetables and assorted herbs around meat. Use another large platter if needed.
3. Place steamboat in the centre of the table. Pour in broth until two-thirds full. When broth starts to bubble, reduce heat to a simmer.
4. Allow guests to cook the beef for themselves. Using chopsticks or fondue forks, each guest dips some beef into egg yolk, then into hot broth. As broth cooks meat, it becomes more flavoursome. When meat is cooked to personal taste, remove from both.
5. Guests can place fresh vegetables, rice vermicelli, cooked beef and assorted herbs into their individual bowls, then ladle broth over. As broth reduces in steamboat, replenish with remaining broth.

Variation

- Prepare broth with vegetable stock and replace beef with a selection of seafood and fish. Use prawns, squid, cuttlefish and cubed salmon fillet.
- Substitute fresh rice vermicelli with dried rice vermicelli or somen noodles. For cooking instructions, see Glossary (Noodles), page 191.

Stung Treng Steamboat

Tch'hav Han Stung Treng

This is a specialty of Stung Treng, a northern province of Cambodia, close to the Laos border. This recipe, a variation of the Khmer steamboat, adds other ingredients such as coconut milk and chillies. The use of chillies shows the Laotian influence, resulting in a spicier dish than the Khmer steamboat. For this recipe, use a steamboat (hot pot) with portable gas stove or hot coals. Alternatively, use a large fondue set over electric hot plates.

Preparation: Average • Cooking: 20 minutes • Serves 4 to 6

Beef fillet 1.2 kg (2 lb 11 oz), sliced thinly

Fresh rice vermicelli 1 kg (2 lb 3 oz)

Round lettuce 2 heads, rinsed, pat- or spun-dry

Bean sprouts 300 g (11 oz), tailed

Cucumber 1, halved lengthwise, then sliced thinly

Fresh aromatic herbs an assorted bunch of fishwort, laksa leaves, mint and sweet basil

Broth

Garlic 5 cloves, unpeeled

Shallots 5, unpeeled

Unsalted peanuts 4 Tbsp, roasted and ground

Dried red chillies 10, soaked, drained, seeded and finely chopped

Prahok 1 tsp, chopped

Prawn (shrimp) paste 1 tsp

Coconut milk 1 litre (32 fl oz / 4 cups)

Salt 2 pinches

Palm sugar 1 tsp

Lime juice extracted from 4 limes or to taste

Fish sauce 2 Tbsp

1. Prepare broth. In a pan, dry-roast unpeeled garlic and shallots over medium heat. When aroma is released and garlic and shallot skins are black, remove from heat. Allow garlic and shallots to cool, then peel skins. Place garlic and shallots in a mortar, then add peanuts, chillies, *prahok* and prawn paste. Pound all ingredients into a smooth paste. Alternatively, use a food processor. Transfer paste to a mixing bowl. Gradually pour in coconut milk, stirring well, until paste has dissolved. Season with salt, palm sugar, lime juice and fish sauce.
2. Arrange beef slices, rice vermicelli, vegetables and assorted herbs on large serving plates.
3. Place steamboat in the centre of the table. Pour in broth until two-thirds full. When broth starts to bubble, reduce heat to a simmer.
4. Using chopsticks or fondue forks, each guest dips some beef into hot broth. As the beef cooks, the broth will become more flavoursome. When beef is cooked to personal taste, remove from both.
5. Guests can place fresh vegetables, rice vermicelli, cooked beef and assorted herbs into their individual bowls, then ladle broth over.
6. As broth reduces in steamboat, replenish with remaining broth.

Variation

- Instead of beef, try this recipe with prawns (shrimps).
- Substitute fresh rice vermicelli with dried rice vermicelli or somen noodles. For cooking instructions, see Glossary (Noodles), page 191.

Saramann Curry

Cari Saramann

Preparation: Long • Cooking: About 2 hours • Serves 4

***Saramann kroeung* (page 41)** 3 Tbsp

Coconut cream 250 ml (8 fl oz / 1 cup)

Beef fillet 600 g (1 lb 5¹/₃ oz), cut into 5-cm (2-in) cubes

Coconut milk 400 ml (13¹/₃ fl oz / 1²/₃ cups)

Whole unsalted peanuts 100 g (3¹/₂ oz), roasted

Palm sugar 2 Tbsp

Fish sauce 2 Tbsp

Tamarind juice (page 35) 2 Tbsp, extracted from tamarind pulp

1. In a pot, dissolve *saramann kroeung* in coconut cream over low heat, stirring occasionally until aroma is released.
2. Add beef chunks and cook for 10 minutes, then pour over coconut milk.
3. Bring to the boil, then reduce heat and simmer over low heat for about 10 minutes. Add remaining ingredients and continue simmering until meat and peanuts are tender and sauce has thickened. Remove from heat.
4. Serve with steamed rice or slices of baguette bread.

Charcoal-grilled Beef Skewers with Lemongrass

Sach Kô Kroeung Chranourch

Preparation: Short • Marinating: 30 minutes • Cooking: 5 minutes • Serves 4 to 6

Beef fillet 1 kg (2 lb 3 oz), sliced thinly

Bamboo skewers as needed, soaked in water

Marinade

Yellow *kroeung* (page 39) 3 Tbsp

Kaffir lime leaves 1 Tbsp, centre vein removed and cut into fine strips

Cooking oil 2 Tbsp

Salt 1 tsp

Palm sugar 1 tsp

Unsalted peanuts (optional) 1 Tbsp, roasted and ground

1. In a mixing bowl, combine ingredients for marinade. Add beef slices and mix well to coat meat evenly. Cover and leave to marinate in the refrigerator for 30 minutes.
2. Thread marinated beef onto bamboo skewers.
3. Place beef skewers on charcoal or barbecue or grill and cook on each side, turning occasionally until meat is tender. This will only take about 5 minutes. Be careful not to overcook.
4. Serve immediately with pickled vegetables (page 46) and steamed rice.

Grilled Meat Pattie Rolls Pum Nout Sach Aing Teuk Chhralourk Paem

Preparation: Average • Cooking: 15 minutes • Serves 4 to 6

Minced meat (pork, chicken or turkey breast) 1 kg (2 lb 3 oz)

Garlic 5 cloves, peeled and chopped

Lard (optional) 200 g (7 oz), cut into small pieces

Salt 2 pinches

Sugar 1 tsp

Roasted ground rice (page 33) 3 Tbsp

Starfruit or Granny Smith apples 3, sliced

Green bananas 2, sliced

Pineapple 1/2, peeled, halved lengthwise, cored, then sliced

Round lettuce 1 head, rinsed, pat- or spun-dry

Cucumber 1, sliced

Fresh aromatic herbs an assorted bunch of fishwort, laksa leaves, mint and sweet basil

Rice paper (spring roll) wrappers 1 package, 15-cm (6-in) rounds

Warm water to soften rice paper wrappers

Dipping sauces

Palm vinegar sauce (page 44) 250 ml (8 fl oz / 1 cup)

Sticky rice dipping sauce (page 43) 250 ml (8 fl oz / 1 cup)

1. In a mixing bowl, combine minced meat and garlic. Add lard, salt, sugar and roasted ground rice. Mix well.
2. Heat barbecue or grill to medium-high heat.
3. With damp fingers, shape meat mixture into small balls. Flatten balls with your palms to make round patties. Barbecue meat patties on each side, until golden brown.
4. On a large platter, arrange fruit, vegetables, aromatic herbs and meat patties. Transfer dipping sauces to individual bowls.
5. Allow guests to serve themselves. Dip a sheet of rice paper wrapper into warm water. Lift rice paper up straight away and transfer to a plate. Place a lettuce leaf on rice paper, then add fruit and vegetables. Top with 1–2 meat patties and plenty of aromatic herbs. Roll up rice paper tightly around filling. Fold in opposite sides towards the centre and over the filling. Continue rolling, then press to seal.
6. Serve immediately, with dipping sauces.

Stir-fried Duck with Long Beans and Lemongrass

T'cha Kroeung Sach Tear

A variation of this recipe is to use beef instead of duck and substitute long beans with red, green and yellow capsicums (bell peppers) or add capsicums together with the long beans.

Preparation: Short • Marinating: 10 minutes • Cooking: 10 minutes • Serves 4 to 6

Free range (organic) boneless duck breasts 600 g (1 lb 5 1/3 oz), skinned and sliced thinly

Long beans or French beans a handful, cut into 4-cm (1 1/2-in) lengths

Onion 1/2, peeled and chopped

Kaffir lime leaves 2, centre vein removed and cut into fine strips

Unsalted peanuts 1 Tbsp, roasted and crushed

Marinade

Yellow *kroeung* (page 39) 2 Tbsp

Salt 1 tsp

Fish sauce 1 Tbsp

Palm sugar 1/2 tsp

Cooking oil 2 Tbsp

1. In a mixing bowl, combine ingredients for marinade. Add duck slices and mix well to coat meat evenly. Cover and leave to marinate for 10 minutes.
2. Heat a wok until hot. Add marinated duck and stir-fry very quickly over high heat. Add long beans and onion and cook for another minute. Give the mixture a good stir. When duck is just cooked and vegetables are almost softened yet crunchy, remove from heat.
3. Transfer to a serving plate. Serve garnished with kaffir lime leaves and peanuts.

Crispy Rice and Meat Pancakes Nom Ambèng Mean Snol

Preparation: Long • Resting: 1 hour • Cooking: 30 minutes • Makes 8 to 10 pancakes

Potato 1/2, unpeeled, pricked on the skin side with a fork, to make a potato brush

Cooking oil 2 Tbsp, for greasing the pancake pan

Round lettuce 1 head, rinsed, pat- or spun-dry

Cucumber 1, sliced thinly

Fresh aromatic herbs an assorted bunch of fishwort, laksa leaves, mint and sweet basil

Batter

Rice flour 450 g (1 lb)

Potato flour 4 Tbsp

Turmeric powder 1 tsp

Water 750 ml (24 fl oz / 3 cups)

Salt 2 pinches

Cooking oil 1 Tbsp

Filling

Cooking oil 1 Tbsp

Minced pork 400 g (14 1/3 oz)

Onions 2, peeled and chopped

Dry-roasted grated coconut (page 36) 3 Tbsp

Salt 2 pinches

Bean sprouts 500 g (1 lb 1 1/2 oz), tailed

Dipping sauce

Palm vinegar sauce (page 44) as needed

Unsalted peanuts 4 Tbsp, roasted and ground

1. Prepare batter. Sift rice flour into a mixing bowl. Add potato flour and turmeric powder. Mix well. Gradually add water then oil and stir until batter is smooth and texture is of thin cream. Add salt. Leave batter to rest for 1 hour.
2. Prepare filling. Heat oil in a wok over medium-high heat. Add all ingredients for filling, except for bean sprouts, and stir-fry. Using a spatula, stir frequently to prevent minced pork from sticking together in lumps. When pork is cooked through, remove from heat and set aside.
3. Using the potato brush, lightly grease a large nonstick pancake pan with oil. Place pan over high heat. When hot, pour a ladleful of batter into the centre of the pan. Working quickly, tilt pan to spread batter evenly over the base. When pancake begins to lift from the edges of the pan, spread filling in centre and top with some bean sprouts. Continue cooking until bottom of pancake is golden and crispy. Fold pancake in half and remove from heat. Repeat with remaining batter.
4. Arrange pancakes on a large platter, each separated by a piece of banana leaf or greaseproof paper. Arrange lettuce, cucumber and aromatic herbs on another large platter. Transfer palm vinegar sauce into individual dipping bowls and sprinkle with peanuts.
5. Allow guests to serve themselves. Place a piece of pancake on a lettuce leaf. Top with slices of cucumber and plenty of aromatic herbs. Roll up lettuce leaf and dip into sauce.

Variation

- Instead of making your own pancakes from scratch, a ready made pancake mix sold under the name of Bánh Xèo, is available from some Asian stores. Follow the instructions on the package.
- To make the filling lighter, replace half the minced pork with 200 g (7 oz) prawns (shrimps), cleaned, prepared (see technique, page 207) and chopped.

Pork and Prahok Terrine Prahok Angkor Wat

This is a refreshing dish. It can be served as a starter or main course with steamed rice.

Preparation: Average • Cooking: 30 minutes • Serves 4 to 6

Minced pork 400 g (14⅓ oz)

Prahok 1 Tbsp

Spring onions (scallions) 4, white part sliced, green tops chopped

Garlic 5 cloves, peeled

Shallots 5, peeled and sliced

Eggs 3, beaten

Palm sugar ½ tsp

Salt to taste

Ground white pepper a pinch

Lemon juice extracted from 3 lemons

Lemon zest grated from 1 lemon

Fish sauce 2 Tbsp

Fresh chives 1 Tbsp, snipped

Coriander (cilantro) leaves 1 Tbsp, chopped

1. Process in a food processor minced pork, *prahok*, spring onions, garlic and 3 shallots until smooth. Set aside.
2. In a mixing bowl, combine pork mixture and beaten eggs. Season with palm sugar, salt and pepper. Add lemon juice, lemon zest, fish sauce and remaining shallots. Mix well until smooth. Stir in chives and coriander.
3. Transfer pork preparation into a terrine dish or loaf tin, cover with a lid and steam for 30 minutes. Alternatively, cook in the oven. Pour some water on a baking tray, place terrine dish on top and cook in a preheated oven at 180°C (350°F).
4. Check if terrine is cooked by inserting the blade of a small knife into the middle. Terrine is cooked when the preparation does not stick to the blade. Remove from steamer or oven and allow to cool before placing on a serving platter.
5. Serve warm with steamed rice and a selection of fresh crunchy vegetables such as small Asian round aubergines, carrots, cucumber, water spinach or broccoli.

Coconut Milk and Prahok Dipping Sauce Prahok K'tis

Preparation: Short • Cooking: 25 minutes • Serves 4 to 6

Minced pork 400 g (14 1/3 oz)

Wood apple 2 Tbsp, hard shell cut in half, quantity required scooped out from centre part

Yellow *kroeung* (page 39) 3 Tbsp

Dried red chillies 4, soaked, drained, seeded and finely chopped, or 1 tsp mild chilli powder

Prahok 2 Tbsp

Salt to taste

Palm sugar 1 tsp

Cooking oil 2 Tbsp

Coconut cream 200 ml (7 fl oz)

Pea aubergines (eggplants/brinjals) a handful, dry-roasted

Kaffir lime leaves 2, centre vein removed and cut into fine strips

1. Process minced pork, wood apple, yellow *kroeung*, red chillies and *prahok* in a food processor. Season with salt and palm sugar.
2. Heat oil a saucepan over medium heat. Add pork mixture and fry briefly. Reduce heat and simmer for 10 minutes, stirring occasionally.
3. Gradually pour in coconut cream, then add pea aubergines and kaffir lime leaves. Simmer gently for another 15 minutes. Remove from heat.
4. Serve with steamed rice and a selection of fresh crunchy vegetables such as cucumber, aubergines, green cabbage, water spinach, winged beans or long beans.

Variation

- Wood apple acts as a souring agent. Replace with tamarind juice extracted from tamarind pulp, tamarind powder or lime juice. Adjust amount needed according to taste.

Stir-fried Vermicelli with Vegetables T'cha Mi Suor Banlè

Present this dish wrapped in an omelette and folded over like a parcel.

Preparation: Average • Cooking: 15 minutes • Serves 4 to 6

Cooking oil 3 Tbsp

Garlic 2 cloves, peeled and chopped

Minced pork 150 g (5$^1/_3$ oz)

Dried black fungus 5, soaked in lukewarm water to soften for 20 minutes, drained, hard stems removed and sliced thinly

Fish sauce 1 tsp

Light soy sauce 1 tsp

Salt to taste

Ground white pepper to taste

Sugar to taste

Carrots 2, peeled and julienned

Courgettes (zucchinis) 2, peeled and julienned

Onion 1, peeled and sliced lengthwise

Mung bean vermicelli (glass noodles) 2 handfuls, soaked in lukewarm water to soften for 10 minutes, drained and cut into 4-cm (1$^1/_2$-in) lengths

Water 100 ml (3$^1/_2$ fl oz)

Fresh chives 1 tsp, snipped

Coriander (cilantro) leaves a few sprigs

1. Heat oil in wok over medium heat. Add garlic and brown lightly. Add minced pork and black fungus and stir-fry until pork is just cooked. Season with fish sauce, light soy sauce, salt, pepper and sugar. Stir well to prevent pork from sticking together in lumps.
2. Add carrots, courgettes, onion, vermicelli and pour in a little water. Reduce heat and simmer gently for 2 minutes, uncovered, stirring occasionally. When vegetables are softened, remove from heat.
3. Transfer to a serving plate and serve hot, garnished with chives and coriander.

Variation

- Replace minced pork with other minced meat such as beef, chicken, turkey or veal. Prawns (shrimps) can also be substituted.
- For a vegetarian option, only use vegetables and increase the amount of vermicelli.

Caramel Pork with Boiled Eggs *Khar Sach Chrouk Pong Tear*

Preparation: Short • Cooking: 45 minutes • Serves 4 to 6

Garlic 4 cloves, peeled

Coriander (cilantro) roots 6, finely grated

White peppercorns ½ tsp

Cooking oil 1 Tbsp

Dark soy sauce 2 Tbsp

Palm sugar 1 Tbsp

Salt 2 pinches

Pork belly with rind or pork shoulder 600 g (1 lb 5⅓ oz), cut in 5-cm (2-in) cubes

Water 200 ml (7 fl oz)

Hard-boiled eggs 6, peeled

Coriander (cilantro) leaves a handful

1. Place garlic, coriander roots and white peppercorns in a mortar and pound. Alternatively, use a food processor.
2. Heat oil in a large pot. Add pounded ingredients and roast until aroma is released. Season with dark soy sauce, palm sugar and salt. Reduce heat to low and cook, stirring until sugar has dissolved and caramelised.
3. Add pork and water. Adjust seasoning and cook over medium heat for 30 minutes.
4. Carefully add boiled eggs and cook for another 10 minutes or until meat is tender. Remove from heat.
5. Ladle into a large serving bowl, garnish with coriander and serve hot with steamed rice.

Grilled Aubergines with Pork Trâb Chienn Sach Chrouk

Preparation: Short • Cooking: 25 minutes • Serves 4 to 6

Asian aubergines (eggplants/brinjals) 6, medium
Cooking oil 2 Tbsp
Garlic 2 cloves, peeled and chopped
Spring onions (scallions) or shallots 3, chopped
Minced pork 200 g (7 oz)
Fish sauce 1 Tbsp
Ground white pepper 2 pinches
Eggs 2, beaten
Coriander (cilantro) leaves a few sprigs, chopped
Fresh chives 1 tsp, snipped

1. Grill aubergines for 15 minutes in a 240°C (465°F) oven until skin is black and flesh is soft. Peel off and discard skins. Set aside flesh.
2. Heat oil in a wok over medium-high heat. Add garlic, spring onions and minced pork. Stir-fry over high heat for 10 minutes or until pork is just cooked through. Stir frequently to prevent pork from sticking together in lumps. Season with fish sauce and pepper.
3. Add aubergine flesh and beaten eggs. Toss ingredients to mix evenly before removing from heat.
4. Serve immediately, garnished with coriander and chives.

Variation

- Replace minced pork with other minced meat such as beef, chicken, turkey or veal.

Salads & Vegetables

Lime-marinated Prawn Salad P'lear Bangkang Teuk Sab

This recipe is a *p'lear*, a salad where raw meat, fish or seafood is cold-cooked by marinating in lime juice. This method keeps the freshness and tenderness of the meat, fish or seafood.

Preparation: Average • Marinating: 20 minutes • Cooking: 5 minutes • Serves 4 to 6

Giant freshwater prawns (shrimps) 6, peeled and deveined (see technique, page 207), sliced

Lime juice extracted from 3 limes

Salt 2 pinches

Garlic 2 cloves, peeled and pounded

Shallots 2, peeled and pounded

Coriander (cilantro) root 1 tsp, grated and pounded

Fish sauce 1 Tbsp

Sugar 1 tsp

Unsalted peanuts 2 Tbsp, roasted and crushed

Fresh aromatic herbs an assorted bunch of holy basil, laksa leaves, mint and sweet basil

Vegetables

Carrot 1, peeled and roughly grated

Red radish 3–4, sliced

Onion 1, peeled and finely sliced

Curly endive (frisée) 1, head, trimmed and torn into bite-size pieces

Bean sprouts 2 handfuls, tailed

Red and yellow capsicums (bell peppers) 1/2 each, white pith and seeds removed, julienned

1. Place prawns in a large mixing bowl. Pour over lime juice and sprinkle over a pinch of salt. Toss lightly to coat prawns evenly. Cover and leave to marinate in the refrigerator for 20 minutes.
2. Squeeze out and collect juice from marinated prawns using your hands. Set prawns aside in the refrigerator.
3. Prepare dressing. Pour juice from marinade into a saucepan. Add garlic, shallots, coriander root, fish sauce, sugar and remaining salt. Simmer for 5 minutes over low heat. Remove from heat and transfer to a bowl. Sprinkle with peanuts and allow to cool.
4. In a large mixing bowl, combine vegetables and prawns. Pour over some of the dressing and toss lightly to mix well. Transfer remaining dressing to a small serving bowl.
5. Arrange salad on a large platter, garnish with aromatic herbs and serve with remaining dressing on the side.

Lime-marinated Beef Salad with Capsicum P'lear Sach Kô M'tés Plaork

Preparation: Average • Marinating: 20 minutes • Cooking: 5 minutes • Serves 4 to 6

Lime juice extracted from 3 limes

Galangal 1 tsp, peeled and chopped

Garlic 3 cloves, peeled and pounded

Salt 1 tsp

Beef fillet 300 g (11 oz), sliced thinly

Fish sauce 1 Tbsp

Sugar 1 tsp

Unsalted peanuts 3 Tbsp, roasted and crushed

Round lettuce 1 head, rinsed, pat- or spun-dry

Red and yellow capsicums (bell peppers) 1 each, white pith and seeds removed, julienned

Lemongrass stalks 2, sliced very thinly

Fresh aromatic herbs an assorted bunch of holy basil, laksa leaves, mint and sweet basil

1. In a mixing bowl, combine lime juice, galangal, garlic and a pinch of salt. Add beef and toss lightly to coat evenly. Cover and leave to marinate for 20 minutes in the refrigerator.
2. Squeeze out and collect juice from marinated beef using your hands. Set beef aside in the refrigerator.
3. Prepare dressing. Pour juice from marinade into a saucepan, add fish sauce, sugar and remaining salt. Simmer for 5 minutes over low heat. Remove from heat and transfer to a serving bowl. Sprinkle with peanuts and allow to cool.
4. In a large mixing bowl, combine lettuce, capsicums, lemongrass and beef. Pour over some of the dressing and toss lightly to mix well. Transfer remaining dressing to a small serving bowl.
5. Arrange salad on a large platter, garnish with aromatic herbs and serve with remaining dressing on the side.

Lime-marinated Fish Salad P'lear Trey

In Cambodia, black sharkminnow (*trey kaek*), a freshwater fish, is used to prepare this dish.

Preparation: Average • Marinating: 20 minutes • Cooking: 5 minutes • Serves 4 to 6

Lime juice extracted from 3 limes

Galangal 1 tsp, roasted and pounded

Garlic 2 cloves, peeled and chopped

Salt 2 pinches

Firm white-fleshed fish fillets 400 g (14⅓ oz), skinned, boned and cut into fine strips

Fish sauce 1 Tbsp

Sugar 1 tsp

Unsalted peanuts 2 Tbsp, roasted and crushed

Fresh aromatic herbs an assorted bunch of holy basil, laksa leaves, mint and sweet basil

Fresh bird's eye chilli 1, seeded and sliced

Vegetables

Onion 1, peeled and sliced thinly

Shallots 1 Tbsp, peeled and sliced thinly

Curly endive (frisée) 1 head, trimmed and torn into bite-size pieces

Bean sprouts 200 g (7 oz), tailed

Red capsicum (bell pepper) 1, white pith and seeds removed, julienned

Lemongrass stalks 2, sliced very thinly

1. In a mixing bowl, combine lime juice, galangal, garlic and a pinch of salt. Add sliced fish and toss lightly to coat evenly. Cover and leave to marinate for 20 minutes in the refrigerator.
2. Squeeze out and collect juice from marinated fish using your hands. Set fish aside in the refrigerator.
3. Prepare dressing. Pour juice from marinade into a saucepan. Add fish sauce, sugar and remaining salt. Simmer for 5 minutes over low heat. Adjust seasoning. Remove from heat and transfer to a serving bowl. Sprinkle with peanuts and allow to cool.
4. In a large mixing bowl, combine vegetables and fish. Pour over some of the dressing and toss lightly to mix well. Transfer remaining dressing to a small serving bowl.
5. Arrange salad on a large platter, garnish with aromatic herbs and sliced chilli. Serve with remaining dressing on the side.

Pomelo Salad Gnoam Krauch T'long

Pomelo is the biggest citrus fruit. In Cambodia, there are two varieties, a sweet kind, used in desserts and a sour kind, used in salads. Both are juicy. The flesh varies from pale-yellow to pale-pink. Grapefruit makes a good substitute.

Preparation: Average • Cooking: 20 minutes • Serves 4 to 6

Pomelos 2, large

Pork belly without rind 300 g (11 oz)

Red capsicum (bell pepper) 1/2, white pith and seeds removed, julienned

Dried prawns (shrimps) 3 Tbsp, soaked in lukewarm water for 10 minutes, then drained and coarsely pounded

Lime juice sauce (page 43) 150 ml (5 fl oz)

Fresh aromatic herbs an assorted bunch of mint, fishwort, laksa leaves and sweet basil

Unsalted peanuts 3 Tbsp, roasted and crushed

Fried sliced garlic (page 34) as desired

Fried sliced shallots (page 34) as desired

Dry-roasted grated coconut (page 36) 3 Tbsp

1. Using a paring knife, peel off thick rind and white pith of pomelos, then separate pomelos into segments. With your fingers, peel away bitter membranes from pulp. Discard membranes and remove pips. Break pulp into bite-size pieces.
2. Bring a large pot of water to the boil and add pork belly. Cook for 20 minutes or until meat is cooked through. Remove from heat and slice pork thinly.
3. In a large salad bowl, combine sliced pork, capsicum and dried prawns. Add lime juice sauce gradually, tasting each time and adjusting the quantity added according to the sourness of pomelos.
4. Add pomelo pulp. Toss lightly to mix well all ingredients.
5. Serve salad garnished with fresh aromatic herbs. Sprinkle peanuts, fried sliced garlic and shallots on top. Add dry-roasted grated coconut last.

Cucumber Salad Gnoam Tra'sak

Preparation: Long • Cooking: 15 minutes • Serves 4 to 6

Pork belly without rind 250 g (9 oz)

Cucumbers 2 (see technique, page 210)

Lime juice sauce (page 43) 150 ml (5 fl oz)

Mung bean vermicelli (glass noodles) a handful, soaked in lukewarm water to soften for 10 minutes, drained and cut in 5-cm (2-in) lengths

Red onion 1/2, peeled and sliced

Red capsicum (bell pepper) 1/2, white pith and seeds removed, julienned

Dried prawns (shrimps) 3 Tbsp, soaked in lukewarm water for 10 minutes, drained and coarsely pounded

Fresh aromatic herbs an assorted bunch of holy basil, laksa leaves, mint and sweet basil

Unsalted peanuts 2 Tbsp, roasted and crushed

1. Bring a pot of water to the boil and add pork belly. Cook for 15 minutes or until meat is cooked through. Remove from heat and slice pork thinly.
2. Cut cucumbers into 5-cm (2-in) sections. For each section, peel cucumber skin in a continuous strip, using a paring knife. Roll skin up and slice it crosswise into fine strips. Set aside. Use the same peeling and slicing technique for cucumber flesh. Discard seeds.
3. Mix lime juice sauce into sliced pork. Add vermicelli, red onion and capsicum and mix well. Add dried prawns last. Toss all ingredients together.
4. Arrange salad on a large serving plate. Garnish with fresh aromatic herbs and sprinkle peanuts on top.

Banana Flower Salad Gnoam Trayong Chek

Preparation: Average • Cooking: 15 minutes • Serves 4 to 6

Banana flowers (blossoms) 2

Water mixed with juice of 1 lemon 250 ml (8 fl oz / 1 cup), for soaking banana flowers

Free range (organic) chicken breasts 2, boiled in lightly salted water and finely shredded

Onion 1, peeled and sliced

Bean sprouts 2 handfuls, tailed

Red capsicum (bell pepper), optional 1/2, white pith and seeds removed, julienned

Lime juice sauce (page 43) 200 ml (7 fl oz)

Fresh aromatic herbs an assorted bunch of mint, fishwort, laksa leaves and sweet basil

Unsalted peanuts 2 Tbsp, roasted and crushed

1. Peel off and discard tough purple outer layers of banana flower. Keep some to be used as decorative food holders for prepared salad, if desired. Discard any yellow undeveloped bananas hidden between each petal. Continue to peel until reaching a layer of white-yellowish petals. These inner petals are tender and suitable for cooking. Cut banana flower in half lengthwise. Remove and discard hard core, then slice banana flower very thinly. To prevent slices from browning, soak in acidulated water as you cut them.
2. Prepare chicken breasts and vegetables.
3. Drain and pat dry banana flower slices.
4. Mix lime juice sauce into shredded chicken. Add vegetables, then banana flower slices. Toss to mix well.
5. Arrange salad on a large platter, garnish with fresh aromatic herbs and sprinkle peanuts on top.

Green Papaya Salad Gnoam L'hong

Unripe papaya or green papaya is used in salads, soups and even stir-fries in the Cambodian countryside. For this recipe, pick a fruit that is nearly ripe. The skin should just have turned yellow and the flesh should still be crunchy.

Preparation: Average • Cooking: 15 minutes • Serves 4 to 6

Pork belly without rind 200 g (7 oz)

Lime juice sauce (page 43) 5 Tbsp

Green papaya 1, peeled, seeds removed, shredded

Dried prawns (shrimps) 2 Tbsp, soaked in lukewarm water for 10 minutes, drained and coarsely pounded

Fresh aromatic herbs an assorted bunch of mint, fishwort, laksa leaves and sweet basil

Unsalted peanuts 2 Tbsp, roasted and crushed

1. In a pot, bring water to the boil and add pork belly. Cook for 15 minutes or until meat is cooked through. Remove from heat and slice pork thinly.
2. In a large salad bowl, mix lime juice sauce into sliced pork. Add shredded papaya, then dried prawns. Toss to mix well.
3. Arrange salad on a serving plate, garnish with fresh aromatic herbs and sprinkle peanuts on top.

Variation

- Try this recipe with crabmeat, prawns or shredded chicken.

Green Mango Salad Gnoam Svay Kchei Trey Chhae

Preparation: Short • Serves 4 to 6

Green mangoes 2, peeled and shredded

Shallots 3, peeled and sliced lengthwise

Lime juice sauce (page 43) to taste

Smoked fish 1, dry-roasted to revive flavour and texture, then skinned, boned and coarsely broken up

Dried prawns (shrimps) 1 Tbsp, soaked in lukewarm water for 10 minutes, drained and coarsely pounded

Fresh aromatic herbs an assorted bunch of mint, fishwort, laksa leaves and sweet basil

Unsalted peanuts 1 Tbsp, roasted and crushed

Fresh bird's eye chillies (optional) 2, seeded and sliced

1. In a large salad bowl, mix shredded mangoes and shallots. Add lime juice sauce gradually, tasting each time and adjusting the quantity according to the sourness of mangoes.
2. Add smoked fish and dried prawns. Toss lightly to mix well.
3. Arrange salad on a serving plate and garnish with fresh aromatic herbs. Garnish with peanuts and chillies, if using.

Ambarella Salad Gnoam M'kak

Ambarella (*Spondias dulcis*) is a fruit the size and the shape of a large egg. It is crunchy in texture and a little sour in taste. In Cambodia, many pregnant women crave for this fruit that they eat raw with coarse salt and chillies.

Preparation: Short • Cooking: 15 minutes • Serves 4 to 6

Pork belly without rind 150 g (5¹/₃ oz)

Lime juice sauce (page 43) 5 Tbsp

Ambarellas or Granny Smith apples 6, peeled and shredded

Shallots 2, peeled and sliced

Smoked fish 1, dry-roasted to revive flavour and texture, then skinned, boned and coarsely broken up

Dried prawns (shrimps) 2 Tbsp, soaked in lukewarm water for 10 minutes, then drained and coarsely pounded

Fresh aromatic herbs an assorted bunch of mint, fishwort, laksa leaves and sweet basil

Unsalted peanuts 2 Tbsp, roasted and crushed

1. Bring a large pot of water to the boil and add pork belly. Cook for 15 minutes or until meat is cooked through. Remove from heat and slice pork thinly.
2. In a large salad bowl, mix lime juice sauce into sliced pork. Add shredded ambarellas, shallots, smoked fish and dried prawns. Toss lightly to mix well.
3. Serve salad garnished with fresh aromatic herbs. Sprinkle peanuts on top.

Green Cabbage Salad Gnoam Spei Kdaub

Preparation: Short • Cooking: 10 minutes • Serves 4 to 6

Lime juice sauce (page 43) 250 ml (8 fl oz / 1 cup)

Free range (organic) chicken breasts 2, boiled and finely shredded

Carrots 2, peeled and grated

Green cabbage 1/2 head, shredded

Onion 1, peeled and sliced

Red capsicum (bell pepper) 1/2, white pith and seeds removed, julienned

Fresh aromatic herbs an assorted bunch of mint, fishwort, laksa leaves and sweet basil

Unsalted peanuts 2 Tbsp, roasted and crushed

1. In a large salad bowl, mix lime juice sauce into shredded chicken. Add carrots, green cabbage, onion and capsicum. Toss gently to mix well.
2. Transfer to a serving plate, garnish with fresh aromatic herbs and sprinkle peanuts on top. Serve immediately.

Stir-fried Water Spinach with Soy Beans T'cha Trakuon Sieng

Preparation: Short • Cooking: 10 minutes • Serves 4 to 6

Water spinach 1 bunch

Cooking oil 2 Tbsp

Garlic 3 cloves, peeled and chopped

Salted soy beans 2 Tbsp, drained

Palm sugar $^{1}/_{2}$ tsp

Ground white pepper to taste

Chicken stock (page 34) or water 100 ml ($3^{1}/_{2}$ fl oz)

Shallots 2, peeled and sliced, or 1 small onion, peeled and sliced

1. Wash water spinach and cut into 4-cm ($1^{1}/_{2}$-in) sections. To prevent water spinach from turning brown, soak in cold water. Drain before using.
2. Heat oil in a wok over medium-high heat. Brown garlic lightly. Add water spinach and salted soy beans. Season with palm sugar and pepper. Add chicken stock. Stir-fry briefly.
3. When vegetables are almost softened, yet crunchy, add shallots or onion. Leave to cook for another few minutes.
4. Remove from heat. Garnish as desired and serve immediately.

Stir-fried Vegetables with Oyster Sauce T'cha Banlè Teuk Kiang

Preparation: Short • Cooking: 10 minutes • Serves 4 to 6

Broccoli 200 g (7 oz)

Baby corn 100 g (3½ oz)

Cooking oil 2 Tbsp

Garlic 2 cloves, peeled and sliced thinly

Dried black fungus 1 Tbsp, soaked in lukewarm water to soften for 20 minutes, then drained, stemmed and sliced thinly

Green cabbage ¼ head, shredded

Red capsicum (bell pepper) 1, white pith and seeds removed, julienned

Oyster sauce 1 Tbsp

Salt 2 pinches

Ground white pepper to taste

1. Separate broccoli stems and florets. Trim stems, then peel and slice diagonally. Cut florets into bite-size pieces.
2. Bring a pot of water to the boil and blanch broccoli and baby corn for 1 minute. Drain.
3. Heat oil in a wok over medium heat. Brown garlic lightly, then add black fungus, cabbage and capsicum. Stir-fry briefly over high heat until softened. Season with oyster sauce, salt and pepper. Gently toss to mix well.
4. Remove from heat and serve hot.

Variation

- Try broccolini or ready trimmed tender-stem broccoli, available in well-stocked supermarkets. This vegetable is a cross between common broccoli and Chinese broccoli and has a flavour and texture resembling that of asparagus. It is tender from floret to stem so the whole vegetable can be eaten as such, therefore reducing preparation time.

Rice & Noodles

Sticky Rice with Prawns Baï Damnoeub Muk Bangkang

Originally served at royal banquets, this dish has become very popular amongst Cambodians at weddings and celebrations.

Preparation: Long • Soaking: 3 hours • Cooking: 35 minutes • Serves 4 to 6

Cooking oil 1 Tbsp

Garlic 4 cloves, peeled and chopped

Small prawns (shrimps) 500 g (1 lb 1½ oz), peeled, deveined (see technique, page 207) and chopped

Salt 2 pinches

Heart or ring cake mould (optional) for dish presentation

Kaffir lime leaves 3, centre vein removed and cut into fine strips

Steamed sticky rice

White sticky (glutinous) rice 500 g (1 lb 1½ oz)

Coconut cream 200 ml (7 fl oz)

Salt 2 pinches, dissolved in coconut cream

Saffron a pinch, dissolved in coconut cream, to give rice its distinctive yellow-orange colour

1. Soak sticky rice for 3 hours. Drain, then steam for 25 minutes or until sticky rice is swollen, soft and translucent (see method, page 32).
2. Heat oil in a wok and brown chopped garlic. Add prawns and season with salt. When prawns just turn pink, continue frying until all the cooking juice has evaporated.
3. Spread prawns at the bottom of a cake mould. Add steamed sticky rice, using a spoon to level and flatten.
4. Carefully invert cake mould onto a serving plate. The shaped sticky rice, decorated with the prawns on top, should slip out. Serve garnished with kaffir lime leaves.

Crispy Rice Cakes with Nataing Sauce Nataing

Preparation: Long • Cooking: 20 minutes • Serves 4 to 6

Crispy rice cakes (page 33) 16

Nataing dipping sauce

Cooking oil 2 Tbsp

Garlic 4 cloves, peeled and chopped

Shallots 2, chopped

Coriander (cilantro) root 1 tsp, grated and ground

Minced pork 300 g (11 oz)

Fish sauce 1 tsp

Palm sugar or brown sugar 1/2 tsp

Salt 2 pinches

Small prawns (shrimps) 500 g (1 lb 1 1/2 oz), peeled, deveined (see technique, page 207) and chopped

Coconut cream 200 ml (7 fl oz)

Saffron a pinch

Unsalted peanuts 3 Tbsp, roasted and ground

1. Prepare *nataing* dipping sauce. Heat oil in a wok over medium heat. Fry garlic, shallots and coriander root until aroma is released. Add minced pork. Season with fish sauce, palm sugar and salt. Stir frequently to prevent meat from sticking together in lumps. When meat begins to change colour, add prawns, coconut cream, saffron and peanuts. Stir occasionally and leave to cook for another 15 minutes or until minced pork is just cooked through and dipping sauce has thickened.
2. Transfer dipping sauce into a serving bowl. Place bowl in the middle of a large platter and arrange crispy rice cakes around. Serve immediately.

NOTE

- In the countryside, during festive days, rice crusts with a chive sauce is a favourite among children. The rice is cooked in large cast iron pots, some reaching 1 metre (3.28 feet) in diameter. The pots are placed directly over a wood fire. When the rice is cooked, the golden-brown rice stuck at the bottom of the pots, or rice crust, is removed. The rice crusts, while still hot, are brushed with a chive sauce. This sauce is prepared by heating oil in a wok and browning chopped shallots. The oil is seasoned to taste with fish sauce and palm sugar. Chopped chives are added and the oil is removed from heat.

Chicken with Rice, Kampot-style Baï Moan Kampot

This dish is a speciality of Kampot, a southwestern province of Cambodia. It is about 150 km (93 miles) from the capital city of Phnom Penh and 30 km (18.5 miles) from Kep, a seaside town. Kampot is best known for its seafood and pepper.

Preparation: Average • Cooking: 1 hour • Serves 4 to 6

Whole free range (organic) chicken 1.5 kg (3 lb 4½ oz), giblets optional, cut into 4 pieces

Water 1.5 litres (48 fl oz / 6 cups)

Coarse salt 1 tsp

Long grain fragrant (jasmine) rice 300 g (11 oz), rinsed and drained

Fried chopped garlic (page 34) 1 Tbsp

Lime juice sauce (page 43) 250 ml (8 fl oz / 1 cup)

Young ginger root 1 thumb-size knob, peeled and pounded

Round lettuce 2 heads, rinsed, pat- or spun-dry

Fresh aromatic herbs an assorted bunch of mint, fishwort, laksa leaves, coriander (cilantro) leaves and sweet basil

1. In a large pot, place chicken, chicken heart and gizzard, if using. Cover with water, add salt and bring to the boil. Reduce heat and leave to cook for 20 minutes, skimming off any impurities that rise to the surface. When the cooking is almost over, add liver, if using.
2. Remove chicken meat and giblets from heat. Cut chicken into bite-size pieces and giblets into small chunks. Keep warm.
3. Strain chicken stock.
4. Steam rice according to instructions on page 32 but replace water with chicken stock. When rice is cooked, sprinkle with fried chopped garlic.
5. Prepare a sauce by mixing lime juice sauce with ginger. Divide among individual saucers.
6. Serve chicken with lettuce, aromatic herbs and sauce on the side. Garnish as desired.

Stir-fried Rice with Seafood Baï Lign Kroeung Samot

Preparation: Average • Cooking: 30 minutes • Serves 4 to 6

Long grain fragrant (jasmine) rice 300 g (11 oz), rinsed and drained

Salt 1/2 tsp

Mussels 200 g (7 oz)

Cooking oil 3 Tbsp

Garlic 2 cloves, peeled and sliced

Shallots 3, peeled and sliced

Cuttlefish or squid 200 g (7 oz), prepared (see technique, page 209)

Fresh crabmeat 100 g (3 1/2 oz)

Medium-size prawns (shrimps) 200 g (7 oz), deveined (see technique, page 207), leaving tails intact

Fish sauce 1 Tbsp

Ground white pepper 2 pinches

Coriander (cilantro) leaves and spring onion (scallion) a handful, chopped for garnish

1. Steam rice (page 32), adding salt to the water.
2. Prepare mussels. Using a kitchen brush, scrub mussels and remove tough fibrous beard. Clean thoroughly and drain. Discard mussels with broken shells.
3. In a large pot, bring a little water to the boil. Add mussels and cook until mussels begin to open. Drain and keep warm. Discard any unopened mussels.
4. Heat oil in a wok. Brown garlic and shallots lightly. Add steamed rice, cuttlefish, crabmeat and prawns. Season with fish sauce and pepper. Stir to mix well and leave to cook until prawns turn pink.
5. Transfer to a serving dish and serve hot, garnished with coriander leaves and spring onion.

Variation

- For convenience, use frozen seafood and canned crabmeat. If using canned crabmeat, drain and discard any shell fragments before use.
- Well-stocked supermarkets sometimes offer seafood selection in a pack (prawns, mussels and squid). Follow the instructions on the pack to defrost seafood. Drain before use.

Rice Vermicelli, Kampot-style Nom Ban Chok Kampot

This simple and tasty dish originated from Kampot, a southwestern province of Cambodia, where it is sold as a street snack throughout the day.

Preparation: Average • Serves 4 to 6

Cucumber 1, halved lengthwise and cut into thin strips

Round lettuce a few large leaves, cut into long thin strips

Bean sprouts 2 handfuls, tailed

Fresh aromatic herbs an assorted bunch of mint, fishwort, laksa leaves and sweet basil

Fresh rice vermicelli 2 kg (4 lb 6 oz)

Dried prawns (shrimps) 300 g (11 oz), soaked in lukewarm water for 10 minutes, drained and coarsely pounded

Fresh coconut cream 250 ml (8 fl oz / 1 cup)

Lime juice sauce (page 43) 250 ml (8 fl oz / 1 cup)

Shallots 2, peeled and sliced

1. Arrange vegetables, herbs and rice vermicelli on serving plates. Place dried prawns and coconut cream in separate serving bowls. Sprinkle lime juice sauce with sliced shallots, then place into dipping bowls.
2. Arrange ingredients on the dining table.
3. To eat, place vegetables on a shallow plate, add vermicelli and top with pounded dried prawns. Drizzle with coconut cream and lime juice sauce. Garnish with plenty of fresh aromatic herbs.

Variation

- Fresh coconut cream can be substituted with 200 ml (7 fl oz) canned coconut cream. Boil before use.
- Replace fresh rice vermicelli with dried rice vermicelli or somen noodles. For cooking instructions, see Glossary (Noodles), page 191.

Rice Vermicelli with Green Sauce Nom Ban Chok Samlar Khmer

There are many variations to this recipe. In Cambodia, depending on which vegetables are in season, a variety of young flowers, young leaves and vegetables are used. In the provinces of Siem Reap, Battambang and Kampot, coconut milk is added to the fish stock.

Preparation: Long • Cooking: 20 minutes • Serves 4 to 6

Green sauce

Water 1.5 litres (48 fl oz / 6 cups)

Snakehead murrel 1 kg (2 lb 3 oz), gutted, scaled and cut into steaks

Prahok 2 Tbsp

Fish sauce 1 Tbsp

Coarse salt 1 tsp, or to taste

Green *kroeung* (page 39) 3 Tbsp

Accompaniments

Banana flower (blossom) 1

Bean sprouts 3 handfuls, tailed

Long beans 4, trimmed and sliced thinly

Cucumber 1, sliced thinly

Fresh rice vermicelli 1.5 kg (3 lb 4½ oz)

Chilli powder (optional) 1 Tbsp

1. Prepare green sauce. In a large pot, bring water to the boil. Add fish, *prahok*, fish sauce and salt. Reduce heat and simmer for 10 minutes or until fish is just cooked. Remove fish to a cutting board. Carefully remove skin and bones. Strain fish stock. Set aside fish and stock. Pound fish and green *kroeung* lightly. In a large pot, bring fish stock to the boil. Add fish and *kroeung* mixture. Reduce heat and simmer over low heat for 5 minutes. Remove from heat.
2. Peel off and discard tough purple outer petals of banana flower. Discard yellow undeveloped bananas hidden between each petal. Continue to peel until you reach a layer of white-yellowish petals. These inner petals are tender and suitable for cooking. Cut banana flower in half lengthwise. Remove and discard hard core, then slice banana flower very thinly. To prevent the slices from browning, soak them in water mixed with some lemon juice as you cut them.
3. Ladle green sauce into a large serving bowl. Arrange vegetables and rice vermicelli on separate platters. Place all ingredients in the centre of the dining table.
4. To eat, place a little of each vegetable in bowl. Add cold rice vermicelli, then top with green sauce. Sprinkle with chilli powder, if desired.

Variation

- Substitute snakehead murrel (*trey ras*) with mackerel, mullet or cod. Alternatively, replace whole fish with 600 g / 1lb 4¾ oz fish fillets.
- If the taste of *prahok* is too strong, use fish sauce or salt.
- Substitute banana flower with 3 grated carrots.
- Fresh rice vermicelli can be substituted with dried rice vermicelli or somen noodles. For cooking instructions, see Glossary (Noodles), page 191.

Stir-fried Rice Noodles with Chinese Broccoli T'cha Kuteav Khatna

Preparation: Short • Cooking: 10 minutes • Serves 4 to 6

Light soy sauce 1 tsp

Oyster sauce 1 tsp

Beef fillet 400 g (14 1/3 oz), sliced thinly

Cooking oil 5 Tbsp

Fresh rice noodles, round or flat 400 g (14 1/3 oz)

Salt 2 pinches

Garlic 2 cloves, peeled and crushed

Chinese broccoli (*kai lan*) 200 g (7 oz), stalks and leaves cut into 5-cm (2-in) lengths, with stalks and leaves kept separate

Bean sprouts 200 g (7 oz), tailed

Onion 1, peeled and quartered

Red capsicum (bell pepper) 1/2, white pith and seeds removed, julienned

Ground white pepper a pinch

Coriander (cilantro) leaves a handful

1. In a mixing bowl, combine soy sauce with oyster sauce. Add beef slices and mix well to coat meat evenly. Leave to marinate.
2. In a wok, heat 3 Tbsp oil over medium-high heat. Stir-fry rice noodles for 5 minutes. Season with salt. Remove from heat and transfer to a serving plate. Keep warm.
3. Heat remaining oil in the wok. Add garlic and beef with marinade juices and stir-fry briefly over high heat. Add Chinese broccoli stalks, bean sprouts, onion and red capsicum. Add Chinese broccoli leaves last. Season with pepper and continue to cook until vegetables are just tender, yet crunchy. Remove from heat.
4. Arrange meat and vegetables over rice noodles. Serve immediately, garnished with coriander leaves.

Variation

- Fresh rice noodles can be substituted with *udon* noodles. See Glossary (Noodles), page 191. Cook according to instructions on the package.
- Replace beef with prawns (shrimps). Clean and devein prawns (see technique, page 207), leaving tails intact.

Crispy Rice Vermicelli with Garnish Mi Bam Pong

Preparation: Long • Cooking: 50 minutes • Serves 4 to 6

Pork mixture

Cooking oil 2 Tbsp

Garlic 4 cloves, peeled and chopped

Shallots 4, peeled and chopped

Dried red chillies 3, soaked, drained, seeded and finely chopped

Pork belly without rind 400 g ($14\frac{1}{3}$ oz), julienned

Pickled garlic (available in Asian stores) 1 Tbsp, sliced

Salted soy beans 1 Tbsp, drained and chopped

Fish sauce 1 Tbsp

Sugar 1 tsp

Salt to taste

Firm bean curd (tofu) 200 g (7 oz), fried and julienned

White wine vinegar 1 Tbsp

Crispy rice vermicelli

Cooking oil for deep-frying 500 ml (16 fl oz / 2 cups)

Dried rice vermicelli 400 g ($14\frac{1}{3}$ oz)

Vegetables

Bean sprouts 500 g (1 lb $1\frac{1}{2}$ oz), tailed

Red capsicum (bell pepper) 1, white pith and seeds removed, julienned

Garlic chives or chives 1 bunch

Garnish

Lemon 1, quartered

Omelette (page 37) 1, sliced into thin strips

Coriander (cilantro) leaves a handful

1. Prepare pork mixture. In a wok, heat oil over medium-high heat. Fry garlic, shallots and chillies until fragrant. Add pork belly, pickled garlic and salted soy beans. Season with fish sauce, sugar and salt. Add fried bean curd. Reduce heat and cook over medium heat until pork is just cooked through. When cooking is almost over, add white wine vinegar and adjust seasoning.
2. To make crispy rice vermicelli, heat oil in a wok. Add vermicelli in small quantities and deep-fry until crisp but not golden brown. Remove immediately using a mesh strainer. Drain on kitchen paper.
3. In a large mixing bowl, toss together crispy rice vermicelli, pork mixture and vegetables. Transfer to a large serving plate. Garnish with lemon, omelette strips and coriander leaves.

Desserts

Sticky Rice in Coconut Milk with Palm Fruit Babar Tnaot

Preparation: Average • Soaking: 30 minutes • Cooking: 30 minutes • Serves 4 to 6

White sticky (glutinous) rice 2 handfuls, soaked in warm water for 30 minutes and drained

Palm juice 1 litre (32 fl oz / 4 cups)

Coconut milk 400 ml (13¹/₃ fl oz / 1²/₃ cups)

Fresh young palm fruit or canned palm fruit 10, peeled and cut vertically into thick slices

Salt 2 pinches

Coconut cream 3 Tbsp, for topping

1. Place sticky rice in a pot, cover with palm juice and bring to the boil. Reduce heat and simmer for 30 minutes until rice is soft and translucent. Stir in coconut milk, palm fruit and salt. Leave to cook for another few minutes.
2. Remove from heat. Scoop into individual cups and top with coconut cream.

Variation

- If using canned palm fruit, wash and drain to remove the syrup before slicing the fruit.
- Substitute palm juice with sugar syrup made by dissolving 8 Tbsp sugar in 1 litre (32 fl oz / 4 cups) water.

Sticky Rice Balls Filled with Palm Sugar Nom Plè Aye

Preparation: Average • Cooking: 25 minutes • Serves 4 to 6

Banana leaves a few, to make banana leaf cups

Sticky (glutinous) rice flour 200 g (7 oz)

Water 150 ml (5 fl oz)

Palm sugar 400 g (14¹/₃ oz), cut in small cubes

Cold water about 1 litre (32 fl oz / 4 cups)

Freshly grated coconut a handful

1. Prepare small banana leaf cups (page 216).
2. To make dough, place rice flour in a large mixing bowl. Gradually pour in water and knead until dough is smooth and malleable. If dough does not come together, the mixture is too dry. Add a little more water. If dough sticks to your hands, it is too wet. Adjust with more flour.
3. Roll dough into 2-cm (³/₄-in) diameter balls. Flatten a ball of dough and place a cube of palm sugar in the centre. Bring edges of dough up over palm sugar, then roll dough into a ball. Repeat until dough and palm sugar are used up.
4. Bring a large pot of water to the boil and cook rice balls in small batches. When balls float, remove with a slotted spoon and place in a basin of cold water to prevent them from sticking together while cooking the rest.
5. Drain rice balls, then roll in grated coconut to coat. Place into banana leaf cups and serve immediately.

Pumpkin Coconut Flan Sankhya L'peuv

This dessert is served for special events and celebrations. It is best prepared the day before and stored in the refrigerator overnight.

Preparation: Short • Cooking: 45 minutes • Serves 4 to 6

Small ripe pumpkin 1, about 15-cm (6-in) in diameter

Eggs 6

Palm sugar or sugar 350 g (12 oz)

Salt 1 tsp

Coconut cream 200 ml (7 fl oz)

1. Using a sharp knife, trim top off pumpkin. Set aside. Scoop out and discard seeds and fibres. Clean pumpkin cavity and leave to drain upside down.
2. In a mixing bowl, break eggs, add palm sugar, salt and coconut cream. Whisk lightly and not too briskly to prevent air bubbles from forming. Strain flan mixture through a sieve to eliminate lumps.
3. Pour flan mixture into pumpkin and cover with pumpkin top. Steam for 45 minutes over medium heat. To check if it is cooked through, insert the blade of a knife or skewer into the centre of the flan. The knife or skewer should come out clean.
4. Remove from heat and allow to cool completely. Refrigerate for at least 10 hours. Serve chilled, sliced into thin wedges.

Bananas in Coconut Milk with Tapioca Chek K'tis

For this recipe, the key is to choose bananas that are just ripe. If the bananas are too ripe, they tend to get mushy when cooked. In Cambodia, *namvar* bananas are used. These are a variety of small bananas that are easy to find in the markets, economical and very sweet when ripe. Use any variety of nearly ripe bananas or very ripe plantain bananas. Steamed sticky rice (page 32) pairs well with this delicious dessert.

Preparation: Short • Soaking: 15 minutes • Cooking: 20 minutes • Serves 4 to 6

Coarse salt 1/2 Tbsp

Just ripe *namvar* bananas 6, peeled, halved lengthwise and cut crosswise into 3 or 4 sections each

Coconut cream 400 ml (13 1/3 fl oz / 1 2/3 cups); set aside 3 Tbsp for topping

Sugar 2 Tbsp or to taste

Salt 2 pinches

Small tapioca pearls 1 Tbsp, rinsed and soaked in warm water

Peeled and split yellow mung beans 1 Tbsp, soaked and dry-roasted

1. In a large bowl, dissolve coarse salt in water. Add cut bananas and leave to soak for 15 minutes. Wash and drain.
2. Pour coconut cream into a pan, add sugar, salt and bananas. Bring to the boil. Reduce heat to low and add tapioca pearls. Leave to cook, stirring occasionally until tapioca is soft and translucent. Remove from heat.
3. Ladle into bowls. Serve with reserved coconut cream and mung beans.

Sticky Rice Cakes with Coconut Filling Nom Kom

These sticky rice cakes with coconut filling are ceremonial cake desserts served at weddings and celebrations. With its triangular shape, soft texture and sweet and moist filling, *nom kom* symbolises womanhood for Cambodians. In the villages, the women would gather to prepare *nom kom* for weddings and other celebrations. Once, I was visiting with my daughter a relative in Dèk Chho. This is a village located on an island beyond the Quatre Bras (Four Arms) confluence. There, the Mekong and the Tonle Sap rivers join and their waters split into the Mekong and the Bassac. We had the opportunity to watch three generations of women, from grandmothers to little girls, making *nom kom* under their traditional stilt-houses.

Sticky (glutinous) rice flour

Water

Palm sugar

Fresh grated coconut

Salt

Sesame seeds

Banana leaves cut into round shapes and greased with oil

Toothpicks

1. To make the dough, place sticky rice flour in a large mixing bowl. Gradually pour in water, add a little palm sugar and knead until dough is smooth and malleable. If dough does not come together, it is too dry. Add more water. If dough sticks to your hands, it is too wet. Adjust with more flour. Leave dough to stand for 30 minutes.
2. Meanwhile, prepare filling. Heat a brass pan, then dissolve palm sugar in a little water over low heat. Add grated coconut and salt. Simmer over low heat, stirring frequently until grated coconut is sticky and has absorbed all the sugar. Remove from heat. Sprinkle with sesame seeds and allow to cool.
3. Smoke filling (see technique, page 215). This is optional but smoking imparts a unique, distinctive flavour to the dessert.
4. Grease your hands with oil, then take a piece of dough and roll it between your palms to form a ball about 4-cm (1½-in) in diameter. Flatten ball and place coconut filling in the centre. Bring edges of dough up over filling and seal by pinching sides together. Roll dough into a ball.
5. Shape banana leaf into a cone. Place ball in the cavity, then fold in opposite sides towards the centre and over the ball to enclose it. Secure with toothpicks.
6. Repeat steps until filling and dough are all used up.
7. Steam banana leaf parcels for 15 minutes.
8. Allow guests to unwrap the parcels themselves. Serve at room temperature.

1000

Banana Fritters Chek Chienn

At almost every street corner in Phnom Penh, these tasty crispy snacks can be found sold by street hawkers for around 600 riels. This is an original recipe, complete with the huge quantities, from my cousin Neang Rom who lives in Taluon, my mother's native village in the province of Kandal. My cousin starts making the banana fritters in the morning and sells them every afternoon under the shade of sapodilla trees.

Rice flour 1 kg (2 lb 3 oz)

Eggs 2, beaten

Salt 1 tsp

Water 2 litres (64 fl oz / 8 cups)

Fresh grated coconut 1/2 coconut

Black sesame seeds 1 tsp

Cooking oil for deep-frying

Ripe *namvar* bananas 90

1. Prepare batter. Combine rice flour and beaten eggs in a large mixing bowl. Add salt, then gradually pour in water, stirring constantly until batter is smooth and thick in texture. Add grated coconut and black sesame seeds. Leave to stand.
2. Heat oil in a large wok.
3. Peel a banana and roll it up in a plastic sheet. With your palms, lightly flatten banana. Dip flattened banana into batter, then deep-fry in very hot oil until golden and crisp. Quickly remove from heat and drain on kitchen paper. Repeat steps until batter is used up.
4. Serve immediately.

Sticky Rice Grilled in Bamboo Sticks Kralan Kratie

If you happen to pass by Kratie, a province in northeastern Cambodia known for its attractive riverside scenery and green villages, make a stop at Tmar Kreae. This is a village on the Mekong River, 5 km (3.1 miles) north of Kratie town on road National 377, where villagers have been making *kralan*, a Kratie delicacy, for many generations. As the grilling process is long and must be carefully monitored, villagers start preparing and cooking this snack from midnight. By early morning, the fresh *kralan* would be ready to be sold at stalls along the village main road. *Kralan* is also famous in the provinces of Stung Treng, Battambang and Siem Reap. However, it is said that Tmar Kreae villagers make the best *kralan* in Cambodia, and people now travel from Phnom Penh to buy these delicacies. This is an original recipe provided by the Tmar Kreae villagers.

White sticky (glutinous) rice 10 kg (22 lb), soaked and drained

Fresh grated coconut

Sugar 800 g (1³/₄ lb)

Salt 250 g (9 oz)

Black-eyed peas (beans), optional 800 g (1³/₄ lb)

Bamboo

Coconut husks

1. To make this snack, the villagers use young bamboo, about 5-cm (2-in) in diameter, cut crosswise into 30-cm (12-in) sections. The sticky rice is mixed with grated coconut, sugar, salt and black-eyed peas, then packed into the cavity of the bamboo and sealed with coconut husks. The bamboo is placed over wood fire and slowly grilled for 1 to 2 hours, depending on the size of the bamboo. They are turned occasionally to ensure even cooking. Once cooked, the bamboo sticks are removed from the fire. The burnt outer layer is shaved off and the bamboo smoothened using a sharp knife. The snack is sold in its bamboo container.
2. To eat, remove the coconut husk and peel the bamboo like a banana. *Kralan* will keep at room temperature for up to 3 days and can be stored in the freezer for up to 2 months.

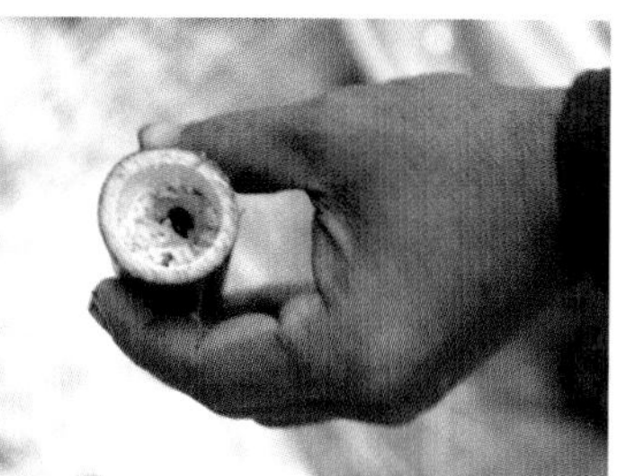

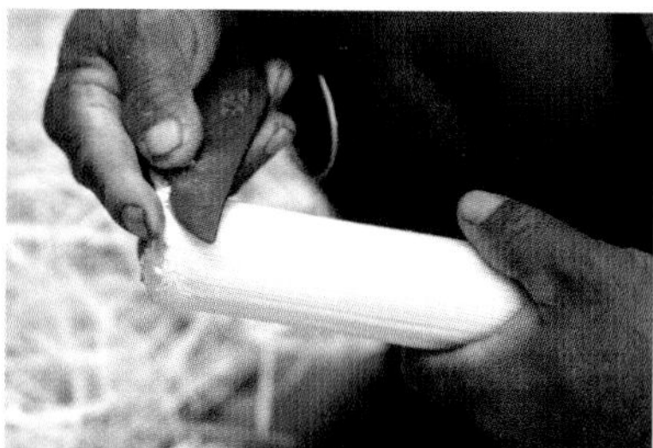

Charcoal-grilled Sticky Rice and Banana Rolls Nom An Sam Chek Aing

Koh Dach or Silk Island is a small island about 15 km (9.3 miles) north of Phnom Penh on the Mekong River. The island is best known for its silk weaving villages. Men and women weave by hand traditional garments in silk such as sampots, sarongs and kramas. To get to Koh Dach, catch the local ferry. Before crossing the Mekong River, stop by Navy's stall, located opposite the ferry pier. The young woman makes delicious sticky rice and banana rolls (*nom an sam chek aing*), grilled on a charcoal fire. Navy starts preparing the sweets in the mid morning to have them ready for the afternoon. Here are the ingredients and quantities kindly provided by Navy. This recipe makes about 80 rolls.

Fresh grated coconut 1.5 kg (3 lb 4½ oz)

Water 3 litres (96 fl oz / 12 cups)

Sugar 500 g (1 lb 1½ oz)

Salt 1 Tbsp

White sticky (glutinous) rice 2 kg (4 lb 6 oz), soaked and drained

Banana leaves for wrapping, wiped with a clean and moist tea towel

***Namvar* bananas** as needed

Bamboo skewers soaked in cold water

1. Prepare homemade coconut milk (page 36) using grated coconut and water. Leave to stand in the refrigerator. Do not discard grated coconut used to make coconut milk.
2. In a large mixing bowl, combine grated coconut, sugar and salt. Mix well and set aside.
3. To make rice filling, skim off creamy part of coconut milk and place in a heavy-based pot. Bring coconut cream to the boil, stirring constantly for 10 minutes. Add sticky rice and continue cooking over low heat, stirring frequently to prevent rice from burning at the bottom of the pot. When coconut cream has been absorbed into rice, add liquid part of coconut milk. Stir until all the coconut milk has evaporated or been absorbed. Add grated coconut mixture and mix well. Remove from heat and allow to cool.
4. Remove tough centre vein from banana leaves and cut leaves into large rectangles. Stack 2 banana leaves together and spread about 2 Tbsp rice filling in the centre. Use a spoon to level and flatten rice. Place a banana on top of rice. Roll rice over banana and wrap banana leaves tightly around rice roll. Close open ends of parcel and secure with bamboo skewers. Repeat until ingredients are used up.
5. Grill on a charcoal fire for 20–30 minutes, turning occasionally to cook rolls evenly.

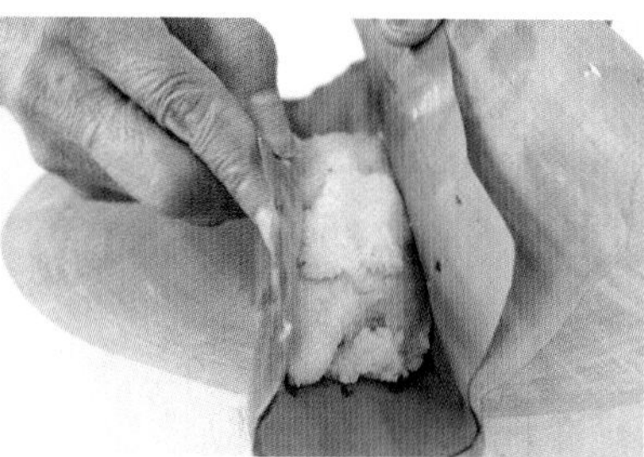

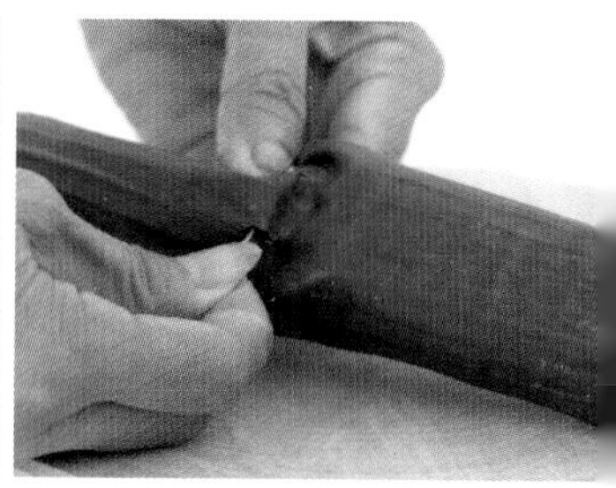

Glossary of Ingredients

A

Ambarella *M'kak*

Ambarella (*Spondias dulcis*) is an oval fruit about 5-cm (2-in) long, with a green skin that turns golden-yellow when ripe. The fruit has a fibrous core that hardens when fully ripe, making it difficult to slice. As such, the fruit is best eaten unripe or nearly ripe. The white flesh is crunchy and a little sour. Sliced raw ambarella is perfect in salads (page 138) and can also be eaten on its own, dipped into a sauce made of *prahok*, palm sugar and fish sauce. When used in cooking, the fruit and leaves impart their sour flavour to the dish.

Aromatic herbs, fresh *T'chi*

Aromatic herbs can be said to be the true taste of Cambodian cuisine which is always fragrant and never excessively spicy. They are indispensable in salads and used to garnish almost every meal such as soups, steamboats and starters.

In recipes, they are used together in an assorted bunch. The quantity of each herb within the assortment differs, depending on your taste and what is available. The key is to strike a balance between the different flavours of the herbs.

The most commonly used herbs in Cambodia are fishwort, holy basil, laksa leaves, mint, sawtooth coriander and sweet basil. In the markets, they are sold together, wrapped in a bunch. Use them quickly as they tend to wilt and lose their aroma rapidly.

To store, wash and drain well the herbs, then wrap in kitchen paper and keep in an airtight container in the refrigerator. It will keep for up to a week.

- **Fishwort** *T'chi thpoal trey*

Grown in moist or wet soil, fishwort (*Houttuynia cordata*) is a heart-shaped leaf with a lemony scent and a tangy taste. Fishwort is mostly used in salads.

- **Holy basil** *T'chi m'reah preuv*

There are two varieties of holy basil (*Ocimum tenniflorum*), a green and a purple one. The purple variety has purple stems and a more pronounced flavour. Both have narrow, serrated leaves which are slightly hairy. The leaves are intensely aromatic with a hot peppery taste. As such it is best used cooked in sour soups and stir-fries but it can be used in salads too.

- **Laksa leaves** *T'chi krassaing tum hum*

Laksa leaf (*Polygonum odoratum*) is a spear-shaped leaf with a coriander-like scent and a strong, hot flavour. It is usually served with other fresh herbs in salads or with summer rolls.

- **Mint** ***T'chi angkam***

Mint has a refreshing scent and taste. If other herbs are not available, opt for a mixed bunch of mint and sweet basil.

- **Sawtooth coriander**
  T'chi banla or t'chi baraing

Sawtooth coriander (*Eryngium foetidum*) has long and narrow serrated leaves which are very tough. The taste and aroma are similar to coriander, but stronger. It is mainly used cooked, in soups.

- **Sweet basil** ***T'chi nieng vong***

Sweet basil (*Ocimum basilicum*) has purple stems and green leaves, with a sweet, peppery scent and aniseed flavour. This is the most common variety of basil used in cooking. Sweet basil is widely used in Cambodian recipes, served as garnish with other fresh herbs.

Aubergine (eggplant/brinjal)

In Cambodia, aubergines come in a wide variety of shapes, sizes and colours. Aubergines tend to discolour quickly when sliced. To prevent discolouration, use a stainless steel knife, then soak the slices in water if not using them straightaway and cook in a stainless steel pot.

Asian varieties are milder tasting than their Western counterparts, except for pea aubergines, the small, pea-shaped bitter variety. Asian aubergines can however turn bitter when ripe. As such, choose young aubergines and use them promptly.

Aubergines can be eaten raw, as a dip. When cooked, it becomes tender and acts as a sponge, absorbing the sauces and flavours it is cooked in.

Aubergine (eggplant/brinjal), Asian
Trab veng

This is the most common variety in Asia. It is elongated in shape and has a light purple skin.

Aubergine (eggplant/brinjal), Asian round ***Trab srouy***

The fruit has the size and shape of a golf ball and comes in different colours, from purple to yellow and white with green stripes. Eaten raw, their crunchy texture and almost sweet taste make the perfect accompaniment to *prahok* dipping sauces and terrines. They are also an essential ingredient in curries and soups.

Aubergine (eggplant/brinjal), pea
Trab put lumgnon

Slightly larger than green peas, pea aubergines grow in clusters. Because of their slight bitter taste, they are best cooked in soups and curries. Pea aubergines go well with dipping sauces made with *prahok.*

B

Bamboo shoot ***Tumpein***

Bamboo shoots are the edible young growth of the bamboo plant. Cone-shaped, they are typically harvested when they are 20 to 25-cm (8 to 10-in) long. Do not eat bamboo shoots raw as they are bitter and hard to digest. Serve them cooked in soups, stir-fries and curries.

Bamboo shoot, canned
For convenience, use canned bamboo shoots. However, canned bamboo shoots are no match for succulent fresh bamboo shoots. If using, remove the processed taste by rinsing and blanching for 5 minutes.

Bamboo shoot, fresh
To prepare fresh bamboo shoots, peel off the tough outer layers to reveal the white core. Slice and boil bamboo shoots until tender, yet still crisp.

Banana, flower (blossom)
Trayong chek

Banana flowers are the cone-shaped, purple buds, hanging at the end of banana clusters.
To prepare banana flowers, peel off and discard the tough purple outer petals and the undeveloped bananas hidden between the petals. Continue to peel until you reach a layer of white-yellowish petals. These inner petals are tender and edible. Cut the banana flower in half lengthwise and remove and discard the hard core. Slice thinly and quickly soak in water with lemon juice, to prevent the slices from browning. Preparation needs to be fast and close to serving time.

Banana flowers can be eaten raw or cooked, in salads or used as an accompaniment to noodle dishes. The taste is slightly bitter.

Banana flowers are also available in dried form. To use, soak the dried flowers in water, rinse and drain.

Banana, fruit *Chek*
The most common varieties grown in Cambodia are *chek namvar*, *chek pong moan*, *chek ambong meas*, *chek snab muk* and *chek nuon*.

Namvar banana is the most popular variety. The fruit is small and very sweet when ripe. It can be found anywhere in the country.

Pong moan banana is another popular variety, smaller than the *namvar* variety. Oval-shaped and sweet, it has a thin golden-yellow skin and flesh.

Banana, leaves *Sleuk chek*
They are used to wrap food for dry-roasting or steaming. Banana leaves are also typically shaped into containers to hold preparations such as fish *amok* (page 74) and desserts.

Before using the leaves, wipe with a clean, moist cloth and cut off the tough centre vein.

Substitute: Parchment paper

Banana, trunk *Dœum chek*

The trunk of a banana plant is formed by several tightly wrapped layers of leaves.

In Cambodia, banana trunk is traditionally used to make *sla thoa*, a ritual object to greet deities at religious ceremonies, weddings and New Year celebrations. The banana trunk acts as a stand, supporting various offerings for deities such as areca nuts, betel leaves, incense sticks and candles. The offerings are held in place on the banana trunk, using small wooden sticks.

The tough outer leaves, which are not edible, are used to wrap and grill fish over a fire or charcoal (page 214). Once the outer leaves have been removed, a white and tender core, about 8-cm (3-in) diameter, remains. This is the edible part of the trunk. The tender core is cut crosswise into 10 to 15-cm (4 to 6-in) long sections and sold in Asian markets.

The tender core is eaten raw as a dip or cooked, served in soups such as banana trunk soup (page 62).

Bean sprouts *Sandek bandos*
see Mung bean sprouts

Bitter gourd ***M'reah***

Bitter gourd (*Momordica charantia*), also known as bitter melon, comes in several shapes and sizes. The most common variety is typically 15 to 20-cm (6 to 8-in) long, light green in colour and with a distinctive ribbed and wrinkly skin. Inside, a thin layer of flesh surrounds a central spongy cavity, filled with large flat seeds and pith. The flesh is crunchy and watery in texture but very bitter in flavour.

There are various ways to reduce the bitterness of this melon. Select young melons and discard the white core and seeds. When eating raw in salads, slice thinly and soak in salted water before using. In soups, leave the vegetable to simmer for a long time.

Bitter gourd, young leaves
Sleuk m'reah

The young leaves of bitter gourd are also very bitter and specifically used for *samlar kâko* soup.

Brick pastry sheets
(*Feuilles de brick*)

These are ready-made pastry sheets, used originally in Tunisia to make brick, a deep-fried filled pastry. The sheets are wafer thin, with a satin sheen to it. When deep-fried, brick pastry is crisper and lighter than rice paper (spring roll) wrappers. Brick pastry sheets are available in the frozen food section of Asian stores.

Bull's horn pepper

Bull's horn pepper (*Capsicum annuum var. corno di toro*) is a 20-cm (8-in) long and narrow sweet pepper, curved like a bull's horn. Red or green in colour, the pepper is sweet and mild in taste. It is delicious served fresh in salads or cooked, roasted or stuffed.

Substitute: Red capsicum (bell pepper)

Cardamom, green ***Kravagn***

An aromatic spice native of South India, cardamom (*Elettaria cardamomum*) was introduced to Southeast Asia more than a thousand years ago. In southwest Cambodia, cardamom still grows on the slopes of the Cardamom Mountains, named after the spice.

Green cardamom is oval in shape and has a papery texture. When split, the pod reveals tiny brownish-black seeds. The pod itself is tasteless, it is the seeds that have a distinctive spicy-sweet aroma, with an intense fragrance.

Cardamom can be bought in the pods, as seeds or ground. As ground seeds quickly lose their aroma and taste, it is best to purchase the pods, then extract the seeds and grind them when needed.

Before extracting the seeds, dry-roast the pods in a pan over low heat to heighten the spice's aroma. Bruise the pods lightly to open them. Remove the seeds and discard the pods. Grind the seeds as required.

Green cardamom is the most common variety. White cardamom is green cardamom that has been bleached white. Black cardamom is another variety, and the pods are larger and have a stronger flavour. Cardamom is an essential ingredient in *saramann kroeung* (page 41).

Chillies ***M'tés***

Chillies come in many shapes, sizes, colours and flavours. On the heat scale, the intensity of chilli ranges from mild to extremely hot. As a general rule, the smaller the chilli, the hotter it is.

Whole chillies, fresh or dried, can be seeded to reduce their fieriness. To do so, cut and discard stalk end. Using the tip of a sharp paring knife, cut the chilli in half lengthwise. Scrape off the white pith and seeds. Afterwards, wash hands, knife and chopping board thoroughly. Do not rub your eyes or lips, during and even after preparing chillies.

Chillies can be bought in various forms: whole or flakes, fresh or dried, powder or purée.

Chillies, bird's eye ***M'tés sras***

Tiny in size yet extremely hot, fresh bird's eye chillies do not need to be seeded. In most recipes, they are optional, depending on individual taste.

When not added to dishes, chillies are served on the side in a small saucer as a condiment. Bruise or slice and add to fish sauce. The leaves can also be used sprinkled on soups.

Stored in vinegar and sealed in glass jars, bird's eye chillies can be kept for several months.

Chillies, dried red ***M'tés kriem***

Dried red chillies should be soaked and seeded before use. Soak in warm water until softened, then drain and remove seeds. The chillies can then be pounded into a paste or sliced thinly. They are an essential ingredient in *kroeungs* and curries.

Chinese broccoli ***Khatna***

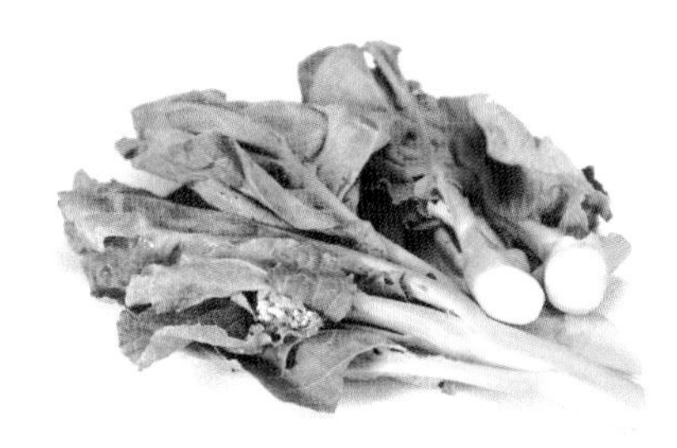

Chinese broccoli (*Brassica alboglabra)* also known as Chinese kale or *kai lan*, has a flavour similar to common broccoli but bitter. The leaves are large, flat and green while the stems are round, crunchy and lighter green in colour. The leaves can sometimes be tough and slightly bitter.

To prepare, pull off and discard the outer leaves and keep only the inner, tender ones. Trim, peel and slice diagonally the stems. Chinese broccoli is delicious stir-fried or steamed.

Substitute: Broccoli

Coconut, cream and milk

Coconut milk adds a creamy and mildly sweet taste as well as smoothness to curries, soups, salads and desserts. Some recipes use both the creamy and the more liquid parts of the coconut milk while others only use the creamy part.

Coconut milk is not the clear liquid found inside a coconut, which is known as coconut water. Instead, it is the liquid extracted from a mixture of freshly grated coconut and lukewarm water. Once the liquid is extracted and left to stand for a while, a thick and white part separates and rises to the top. This is coconut cream. The thinner liquid at the bottom is coconut milk. Both fresh cream and milk are best used rapidly. The extraction can be homemade (page 36), but it is a long process although the taste is incomparable. For convenience, substitute with canned unsweetened coconut milk. Good brands of canned coconut milk have a layer of thick cream while the milk on the bottom will be more watery. Once the can is opened, transfer the coconut milk to a sealed jar and keep refrigerated for up to 4 days.

Coconut, grated

Traditionally, in Cambodia, a special coconut grater (*knâos kâos dông*) is used to make grated coconut. The grater is a low, small wooden stool, carved in the shape of a rabbit or cat, with a grating blade at the end. The person sits on the stool, holds half of a coconut with

both hands, then places it against the blade, making quick and short strokes to grate away coconut meat. There are now hand-held coconut graters available on the market which makes the grating process quicker and easier. Alternatively, remove meat from shell using a knife, peel off brown skin, cut into chunks and chop using a food processor.
Freshly grated coconut is a key ingredient in many desserts. It is also sprinkled over sweets as a coating.

Substitute: Frozen grated coconut or desiccated coconut (also called dried shredded coconut). For desiccated coconut, be careful to buy the unsweetened kind as the sweetened type, most commonly available in the baking section of grocery stores, is not suitable in our recipes. However, nothing beats freshly grated coconut, which is moist, tastier, and crunchier.

Coconut, grated and dry-roasted
Dry-roasted grated coconut is freshly grated coconut, dry-roasted in a wok over low heat until the shreds are dry, aromatic and golden brown.

Used as a garnish on salads, dry-roasted grated coconut adds a crunchy texture and a nutty flavour. Dry-roasted coconut also pairs well with curries. It is a key ingredient in *saramann kroeung*, the paste used in *saramann* curry (page 111).

Coriander (cilantro) ***T'chi van su***

All parts of the plant (*Coriandrum sativum)* can be used from its leaves and roots to the seeds.

Coriander, leaves
With its broad, serrated edges, coriander leaves resemble flat-leaf parsley. However, it has a much stronger, distinctive flavour.

Fresh coriander leaves are widely used to garnish, flavour and add colour to stir-fries and soups. When adding fresh coriander leaves to a hot dish, add them only at the last minute to ensure that their aroma and flavour do not diminish through cooking.

Coriander, root
Coriander roots have a deeper and more intense flavour than the leaves. In Cambodian cooking, they are pounded with garlic and used to season dipping sauces and meat.

Coriander, seeds
About the size and shape of a white peppercorn and golden-brown in colour, coriander seeds are the berries of the coriander plant. They have a warm, nutty and faint orange flavour, which is enhanced when the seeds are dry-roasted before they are ground.

Coriander seeds are frequently combined with cumin seeds. They are dry-roasted and ground together before being used in curries.

Cumin seeds

Small, elongated and brown-yellow in colour, cumin seeds (*Cuminum cyminum*) have a strong, spicy and bitter taste, which is enhanced by dry-roasting and grinding the seeds. Use sparingly as only a little is needed to impart its flavour.

Cumin seeds are often used with coriander seeds as the latter offsets the bitterness of the former.

D

Dried black fungus ***Tra cheak kan dor*** *see* Mushrooms

F

Fingerroot (Chinese keys) ***Khchieay***

Fingerroot (*Boesenbergia pandurata* or *Kaempferia pandurata)* is a member of the ginger family. The rhizome looks like a cluster of long fingers growing out of a centre piece. For that reason, it has traditionally been called fingerroot. It is also known as Chinese keys.

Once scraped off, the orange-brown skin reveals a yellow, tender flesh. Milder than ginger in taste, fingerroot is used in *kroeungs*, soups and fish *amok* (page 74).

The rhizome can be found growing in almost every garden in the countryside in Cambodia.

Substitute: Dried fingerroot. To use, soak dried fingerroot in water, then drain.

Fish

In Cambodia, fish is abundant and varied in supply. Fermentation, salting, sun-drying and smoking are the most important methods of preservation for fish, and this has remained largely unchanged over the centuries.

Fish, dried salted ***Trey ngiet***

Dried salted fish is made by salting freshwater fish fillets and leaving them to dry in the sun. Fish such as *trey pra*, *trey ras* and *trey prama* are very sought-after for salting and they are the most expensive of salted fish. In the countryside, villagers salt whatever fish is available.

Fish, fermented

- **Pha'ak**

Like *prahok*, *pha'ak* is a sort of fermented fish used in soups or simply fried in a pan. *Pha'ak* that is made with big freshwater fish is tastier.

To make *pha'ak*, freshwater fish such as catfish (*trey pra, trey kes* or *trey chhlaing*) or carps (*trey pruol* or *trey chhkok*) are first gutted, scaled and cleaned, then rubbed with coarse salt. The fish is then put into earthenware jars, pressed down with a woven bamboo mat, covered with a lid and left to ferment. This is the first stage of fermentation. The fish is then taken out of the jars, coated in a mixture called *tapè*, which is red or white cooked sticky rice combined with yeast and palm sugar. The coated fish is placed back into the jars and left to ferment again. This is the second stage of fermentation which enables the saltiness of *pha'ak* to be offset by a blend of sweetness and sourness.

Pha'ak can be eaten after just 20 days of fermentation but can be preserved for many months.

- **Prahok**

Prahok is fermented fish paste used widely as a seasoning in Cambodian cooking. Light grey in colour, with no discernible fish chunks, the paste has a pungent smell and a strong and salty flavour. *Prahok* adds depth to many dishes, soups and dipping sauces.

Prahok can also be eaten raw as a dipping sauce. Mixed with palm sugar and a little water or fish sauce, it is served with unripe fruit such as papaya, mango, banana, *kantout* fruit and ambarella.

It is a key ingredient of Cambodian cooking. In the countryside and rural regions, it is often the only source of protein for villagers where a meal simply consists of rice and a little *prahok*.

To make *prahok*, fresh fish, big or small, with or without bones, is used. As a rule of thumb, the larger the fish, the better and thus the more expensive the *prahok* is. However, I find *prahok* made using small fish much tastier. The best *prahok* is said to come from Siem Reap, a province in northwestern Cambodia, on the banks of the

Tonle Sap Lake, where fish is abundant and varied.

There are two sorts of *prahok*, one prepared from whole fish with bones (*prahok ch'oeung*) and another from fish without bones (*prahok sach*).

- **Prahok ch'oeung**

To make *prahok ch'oeung* (fermented fish with bones), small freshwater fish such as *trey kamplieng* or *trey riel* are used. The heads are discarded and the fish gutted and scaled, then left to stand overnight in a little water. The fermentation process is then the same as for *prahok sach* (see below).

- **Prahok sach**

For *prahok sach* (fermented fish without bones), big, meaty freshwater fish are used such as *trey ras* (a sort of snakehead) or *trey kaek* (a type of carp). The heads are discarded and the fish gutted, scaled and boned. The fish are filleted, cut into large chunks and left to stand overnight. The following day, the fish are drained and left to dry in the sun. When dry, they are rubbed with coarse salt and placed in large baskets lined with banana leaves that have been pierced to collect the liquid from the fish. This liquid is used to make fish sauce (*teuk trey*).

Once the liquid is collected, the fish are salted and dried one more time, then put into large earthenware jars. The jars are sealed and the fish are left to ferment for at least 5 months before being used. Just by the smell released by the fish, villagers know, based on their experience, when the fermentation process is over. *Prahok* should be consumed within one year.

Prahok is sold in glass jars labelled as "*Prahok*" or "Fermented Fish Paste". It is available in Asian grocery stores.

Fish, freshwater

Most recipes use freshwater fish because the supply is abundant and varied in Cambodia.

Substitutes are indicated wherever applicable.

- **Catfish**

This is a fish with distinctive barbels around the mouth, resembling cat's whiskers, thus the name. There are many varieties of catfish:

□ Butter catfish / *Trey taon* (*Ompok bimaculatus)*
□ Spot pangasius / *Trey po* (*Pangasius larnaudii*)
□ *Trey chhlaing (Hemibagrus spilopterus)*
□ *Trey kes (Micronema bleekeri)*
□ *Trey pra (Pangasius bocourti*)
□ Walking catfish / *Trey andeng* (*Clarias batrachus*)
□ Wallago / *Trey kropaut* (*Wallago attu*)

- **Featherback**

□ Bronze featherback / *Trey slat (Notopterus notopterus)*
□ Clown featherback / *Trey kray (Chitala ornata*)

- **Snakehead**

□ Giant snakehead / *Trey chhdor (Channa micropeltes)*
□ Snakehead murrel / *Trey ras (Channa striata)*
This is a firm, white-fleshed freshwater fish with few bones. It is a favourite in Cambodian cuisine and is considered the best fish for soups and grilling. The fish is available from Asian stores, labelled as *cá lòc*. Depending on the recipe, snakehead murrel can be substituted with firm white flesh fish or mackerel, mullet, tilapia and cod.

Fish, other freshwater

□ Black sharkminnow / *Trey kaek (Labeo chrysophekadion)*
□ Boeseman croaker / *Trey prama (Boesemania microlepis)*
□ Tilapia / *Trey tilapia*
This is a firm white-fleshed fish with a mild, neutral taste, which means it takes flavours easily. It is widely available and makes a good substitute for snakehead murrel (*trey ras*) and sea bream.

Fish, saltwater

□ Mackerel / *Trey plathou*
□ Silver pomfret / *Trey chap (Pampus argenteus)*

Fish, sauce *Teuk trey*

Fish sauce is a key ingredient in Cambodian cuisine and used extensively as a condiment. A thin and clear golden-brown liquid, fish sauce has a pungent smell with a strong salty taste. Yet, when added to other ingredients, fish sauce imparts its distinctive flavour to various dishes, dipping sauces and soups.

To make fish sauce, fish is rubbed in coarse salt and put into large wooden barrels or earthenware jars. Next, the fish is covered with a woven bamboo mat and weighted down with heavy stones. The barrels or jars are sealed and the fish is left to ferment for many months. The fish is then slowly pressed, yielding the fish sauce, which is then bottled. Cambodian homemade fish sauce contains some additional ingredients such as pineapple skin, dry-roasted galangal and garlic, which are added to the freshly extracted fish sauce. The fish sauce is left to stand, covered, for about 3 months before being filtered and bottled.

Fish sauce is available from Asian stores and well-stocked supermarkets. Labels should read "Fish Sauce". Fish sauce is sometimes referred to by its Thai name (nam pla) or Vietnamese name (nuoc mam). Select a brand that offers a clear, golden brown sauce without any sediment or added ingredients, besides fish, water and salt.

As fish sauce is fermented, it does not require refrigeration.

Fish, smoked *Trey chhae*

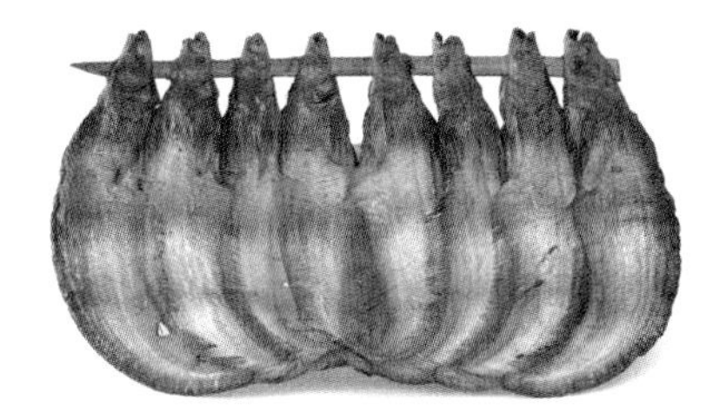

Smoked fish adds its crispy texture to salads (*gnoam*), whilst its smoky flavour is enhanced in dipping sauces and soups.

Smoked fish is made with freshwater fish, usually catfish (*trey andeng, trey kes* or *trey taon*). The fish are threaded by their head onto a strong wooden stick, smoked slowly over a wood fire, then dried in the sun. The process of smoking and sun-drying is repeated until the fish are completely dried and crispy.

Because of the long process, smoked fish is rarely homemade. Hanging above the stalls or stacked in bamboo baskets, it is sold in markets, where people buy them "by the *kras*", literally meaning "by the comb", due to their comb-like shape.

Smoked fish from Siem Reap is considered the best.

Before using smoked fish, dry-roast the fish to revive the taste and texture. Skin and bone, then break into pieces or grind as required by the recipe.

Five-spice powder

This is a mixture of five spices: Sichuan pepper, star anise, cinnamon, cloves and fennel seeds. Brown in colour, fragrant, spicy and slightly sweet in taste, five spice powder is used to season chicken, duck and pork, in particular, spare ribs.

G

Galangal *Romdéng*

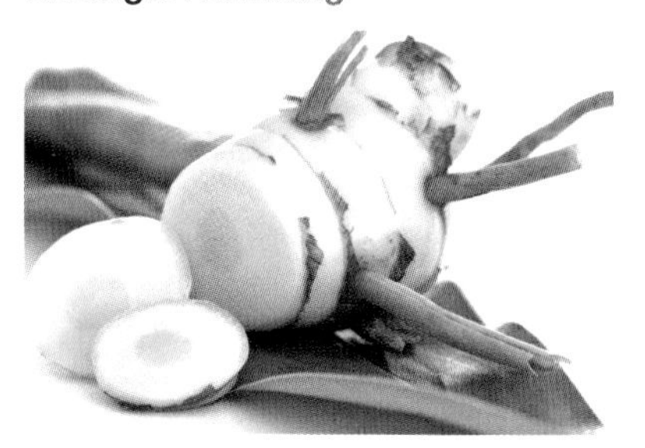

This rhizome (*Alpinia galanga*) is a member of the ginger family. The fresh root has an almost translucent cream-coloured skin and young shoots are pink. The flesh is hard and the taste similar to that of ginger but less pronounced. As the root matures, the skin becomes beige-colored, the flesh even harder and the taste more pungent and peppery.

Galangal is too spicy to be eaten raw. It should be peeled and used sliced, crushed or chopped before being pounded. Galangal is a key ingredient in *kroeungs*. It enhances the flavour of soups and salads.

Store in a plastic bag, in the refrigerator, to avoid drying out.

Substitute: Frozen galangal. Dried galangal is an acceptable substitute for soups. Use powdered galangal for *kroeungs*, salads and dipping sauces.

Garlic ***Ktim sar***

Garlic is widely used in Cambodian cooking. Once peeled, slice clove in half and remove the green sprout (germ), as it has a bitter taste and can be indigestible.

Garlic is used to prepare *kroeungs* and it should always be added last in the pounding process. Garlic is also used to make fried chopped garlic and its perfumed garlic oil (page 34) as well as fried sliced garlic (page 34). Along with a little garlic oil, spoon fried chopped garlic over soups, stir-fries and grilled meat for additional texture and flavour. Sprinkle fried sliced garlic over salads and sauces.

Garlic chives ***Kouchhay***

Garlic chives (*Allium tuberosum*), also known as Chinese chives, are widely used in Cambodia. The stalks, with their flower heads, are long and round. The leaves are somewhat shorter and flat. Both flower stalks and leaves taste like garlic, although less pronounced.

Garlic chives are eaten raw in summer rolls or crispy rice vermicelli with garnish (page 160). They impart their distinctive flavour to noodles and stir-fries.

The leaves and the flower stalks are sold separately in markets. Flower stalks are best when the flower heads are closed.

Substitute: Chives

Ginger ***K'gneï***

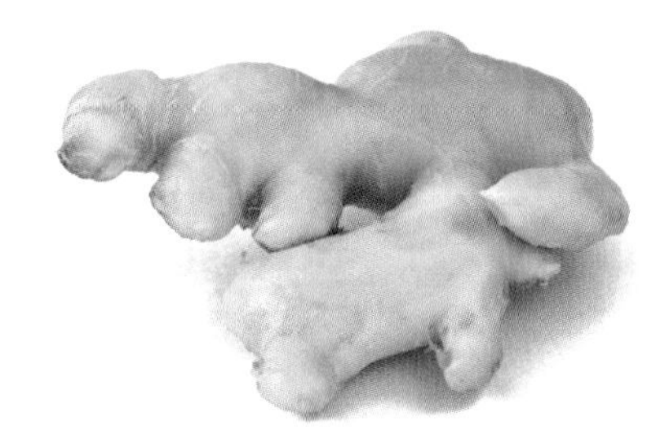

There are many varieties of ginger (*Zingiber officinale*). The two most commonly found in Cambodia are young ginger and mature ginger root. The young root has a translucent pale yellow skin and young pink shoots with green ends. The flesh is tender and juicy with a mild taste.

As the root matures, the skin becomes thicker and turns beige-brown in colour. The flesh is more fibrous and drier and the flavour is more pronounced and pungent. To reduce sharpness, cut ginger, rub in salt and leave to stand for a few minutes. Rinse in water and drain before use.

Always peel ginger before use. Young ginger is best eaten raw as a dip. Mature ginger is best used cooked, ground, julienned or chopped in pickles, dipping sauces, soups, stir-fries and rice dishes. It can also be sliced and used in desserts or crushed to make ginger tea.

Ginger is available in Asian supermarkets. Store in a plastic bag, in the refrigerator, to prevent drying out.

In recipes, always use fresh ginger, unless otherwise specified.

K

Kaffir lime ***Krauch saeuch***

Kaffir lime (*Citrus hystrix*) is a member of the citrus family. About the size of a lime and pear-shaped, it has a dark green, warty skin. In Cambodia, there is a saying, "*Mok akrok doch krauch saeuch*". This literally means that a person with unattractive face features is ugly as the kaffir lime skin.

There is virtually no juice in the fruit. Kaffir lime is mainly used for its intensely aromatic leaves and zest.

Kaffir lime, leaves

Kaffir lime leaves have a characteristic double leaf shape, with a more pointed top leaf joined to a more rounded bottom leaf. Leaves are dark green, glossy and have a lovely penetrating lemon scent. Leaves are used whole to flavour sour soups or are sliced into very thin strips to garnish dishes. Before slicing, always remove the tough central vein.

Kaffir lime leaves can be found in Asian stores. If fresh leaves are difficult to obtain or out of season, buy plenty when they are available and freeze them, sealed in a plastic bag. Before use, frozen leaves should be thawed. If using dried leaves, soak first in warm water. Use fresh leaves as far as possible, as frozen and dried leaves would have lost their colour, flavour and texture.

Kaffir lime, zest

Kaffir lime zest is more aromatic than the leaves, as it contains a high concentration of essential oils. When peeling away the skin, avoid including the white pith which is very bitter. Kaffir lime zest is a key ingredient in *kroeungs*.

Kroeung

Kroeung is distinctively Khmer, giving a unique and aromatic flavour to many dishes such as stir-fries, sour soups, grilled meat, steamed meals and curries.

It is a mixture of several herbs and spices pounded into a smooth paste. The six main ingredients are lemongrass, galangal, kaffir lime zest, turmeric, garlic and shallots. There are five sorts of *kroeung*. These are yellow *kroeung*, green *kroeung*, red *kroeung*, *k'tis kroeung* and *saramann kroeung* (pages 39–41).

L

Leaves *Sleuk*

Bahs leaves (*Sleuk bahs*)

Kantout leaves (Sleuk kantout)

Curry leaves (Sleuk kantrok)

Cambodia is blessed with many fertile regions, "the lands of the gardens and fields" or *srok chamcar*, which provide a wide variety of leaves, used mainly as vegetables in soups.

- **Leaves, for fish *amok***
  - Noni, young leaves / *Sleuk gnor*
    Noni (*Morinda citrifolia*), a plant also known as Indian mulberry, produces large glossy leaves, about 20-cm (8-in) long and 10-cm (4-in) wide. The young leaves are specifically used in fish *amok* (page 74).

- **Leaves, for *samlar kâko* soup**

  Below are the main leaves used specifically in *samlar kâko* soup:
  - Bitter gourd, young leaves / *Sleuk m'reah* (*Momordica charantia*) *see* Bitter gourd
  - Curry leaves / *Sleuk kantrok* (*Murraya koenigii*)
  - Moringa oleifera leaves / *Sleuk m'rom*
  - *Sesbania grandiflora*, young leaves / *Pkar angkear dei*

- **Leaves, other**
  - *Bahs* leaves / *Sleuk bahs*
    This climbing vine grows easily in moist or wet soil across the countryside. The green heart-shaped leaves are used as a vegetable in soups.
  - *Kantout* leaves / *Sleuk kantout*
    These small pointed leaves come from the *kantout* tree and are used specifically for a fish salad (*nem trey*) and bamboo shoot soup (*samlar tumpein sras*). The tree produces clusters of small, round and yellow fruit. The fruit can be sweet or sour, depending on the variety of *kantout*. The fruit is eaten raw with *prahok* sauce.

Lemongrass *Sleuk krey*

Lemongrass (*Cymbopogon citratus*) grows in clumps, each containing several stalks. The stalk is firm and woody with a pale, yellow bulbous base and long, tightly packed, flat green leaves.

The fragrance of lemongrass is subtle until the stalk is bruised, cut or the leaves rubbed. It is a distinctive aromatic lemony scent.

Lemongrass is available in Asian markets and well-stocked supermarkets, although the stalks are easier to find than the leaves. Store in the refrigerator for several weeks or 2 to 3 months in the freezer.

Try growing your own lemongrass as they grow fairly easily in temperate and warm climates. Buy some stalks, place the bulb end in water until roots develop, then plant them indoors in a pot or in the garden.

Lemongrass, leaves

The leaves have a stronger flavour than the stalk. Chopped then pounded, the leaves are a key ingredient and give their characteristic colour to the green *kroeung* paste. Rubbed and added to cooked food, the leaves perfume the dish (pumpkin soup, page 59).

Lemongrass leaves are said to have various healing properties. The leaves, lightly bruised and left to infuse in hot water with sliced ginger and a little honey, make an excellent herbal tea. The infusion is said to help with digestion, cough and colds and support the body's natural defenses. There is a popular Cambodian belief that dew-covered lemongrass leaves brushed over babies' feet can help with a delay in walking.

Lemongrass, stalk

Lemongrass is an essential ingredient in *kroeungs*, imparting its aromatic lemony flavour.

To prepare, remove the outer tough and fibrous layers until the tender, pale pink bulb is revealed. Remove green leaves or reserve if they are called for in a recipe. The yellow part of the stalk can be bruised and added to soups, chopped then pounded into a paste in *kroeungs* or sliced very thinly in salads.

Lime ***Krauch chmar***

This citrus fruit (*Citrus aurantifolia*) is round or oval-shaped with a thin, bright green skin. As limes mature, the skin takes on a slight yellow cast. Limes are similar to lemons but they are smaller, the juice more sour and the zest more aromatic.

A souring agent, lime juice is used extensively to dress salads, season soups and seafood.

Lemon juice is a disappointing substitute as it lacks flavour and aroma.

Long beans ***Sandek kour***

Long beans (*Vigna sesquipedalis*), also known as yard long bean or snake bean, is a climbing vine. The name refers to the length of the pods which can reach 40 cm (15 in) when fully grown. Long beans are similar to French beans in colour and taste but they are stringless.

The pods are best consumed young when they are fresh and crunchy. They can be eaten raw or cooked in soups, curries and stir-fries.

Before use, trim ends and cut long beans into short sections.

Substitute: French beans

Lotus ***Chhouk***

Lotus (*Nelumbo nucifera*) is a water plant growing in the mud of shallow ponds throughout Cambodia. All parts of the plant can be used, flowers, leaves, roots, seeds and young stems.

Lotus, flowers ***Pkar chhouk***
Lotus flowers are large with many petals, ranging from white to pale pink in colour. They are sometimes mistaken for water lilies. Lotus flowers and leaves stand high above the water line whereas water lilies flowers and leaves stay on the water surface.

Lotus flowers, steeped in water for a few hours, produce a delicious perfumed water, very much enjoyed by Cambodians for its soothing properties. Lotus-scented water is also used to perfume desserts.

Lotus, leaves ***Sleuk chhouk***
The wide, disc-shaped leaves are used to wrap food for steaming.

Lotus, roots ***Moeum chhouk***
The roots are firmly anchored in the mud under the water surface. Once peeled, the reddish-brown skin reveals a white, crunchy flesh. The roots are pocketed with air canals so that, when sliced crosswise, they look like discs with tiny holes. To prevent slices from browning, quickly soak in water mixed with lemon juice as you cut them. Lotus roots are delicious in soups.

Lotus, seeds ***Krab chhouk***
Lotus seeds are formed inside a cone-shaped seed head. Young seeds or seeds harvested before they are fully mature, are oval-shaped, with a green outer shell and white, crunchy centre. During the wet season, they are sold daily by street hawkers around Phnom Penh. Along the road to Kompong Cham, where marshes abound, villagers sell them to hungry travellers. The seeds can be eaten raw as a snack. Young green seeds can also be made into an infusion, which is said to help digestion.

When the seeds mature, the outer shell becomes hard and turns brown, then black in colour. The inside has a floury texture and a flavour reminiscent of chestnuts. These seeds are dried, shelled and sold canned or in a package. Choose canned seeds over the packaged ones as the latter requires a long soaking and cooking time.

Lotus, young stems ***Kra av chhouk***
These are the young stems of the lotus plant. In Cambodian markets, they are sold fresh, in looped bundles. Prior to use, the stems should be peeled, cut into sections and their tough fibres removed (technique page 206). With their crunchy texture, they are popular in soups, salads and stir-fries.

M

Mango ***Svay***

Across the country, mango (*Mangifera indica*) trees grow nearly everywhere. There are many varieties of mangoes, from small to large and sweet to sour. Colours range from green to yellow to orange. The fruit is oval, sometimes round, with a flat, fibrous stone. Sour unripe mangoes are used in salads while sweet ripe ones are consumed for desserts.

Mung bean ***Sandek baï***
Mung bean is a legume, the seed of the *Vigna radiata*. The beans are small, oval and green olive in colour. They can be eaten whole, with or without the skin. They should be soaked before being cooked.

Mung bean, sprouts (Bean sprouts)
Sandek bandos

Mung bean sprouts, commonly referred to as bean sprouts, are sprouts grown from mung beans. They should not be confused with soy bean sprouts. Soy bean sprouts have bigger heads and tails that become bitter when they get too long. Mung bean sprouts are crisp and white, with a delicate hint of sweetness. High in protein, they are a vital ingredient in Khmer cooking. Consumed raw or cooked, they feature in many dishes, from salads to stir-fries.

Mung bean sprouts are very perishable and should be used within a day. To keep them fresh and crunchy, store in the refrigerator.

Mung bean, starch

Mung bean starch, extracted from ground mung beans, is used to make mung bean vermicelli, also known as glass noodles because of their translucent appearance, once cooked.

Mung bean starch is also used in desserts, such as *nom ko hev*, a succulent flan, made with coconut milk, sugar and water chestnuts.

Mung bean, vermicelli (Glass noodles) *see* Noodles, fresh and dried

Mung bean, yellow, peeled and split

Once their green skins are removed and the beans split, a yellow inside is revealed. Peeled and split yellow mung beans should be soaked overnight prior to use. Added to soups, they are a good source of protein. Roasted and sprinkled over desserts, they are visually appealing and add a crunchy texture to the dish.

Mushrooms ***Pset***

Recipes in this book call for three main varieties of mushrooms to be used either fresh or dried: black fungus, shiitake mushrooms and straw mushrooms.

- **Dried black fungus**
  Tra cheak kan dor

Also known as cloud ear or wood ear (*Auricularia auricula-judae* and *Auricularia polytricha*), this fungus grows on a variety of woods like mango and kapok trees. The name derives from its ear-like appearance. Brown in colour and prized for its gelatinous and crunchy texture, the fungus has little taste on its own, and absorbs all the flavours it is cooked in. Black fungus is mainly enjoyed in stir-fries, soups and added to meat stuffing and spring roll fillings.

Black fungus is mostly sold in its dried form. Prior to use, soak black fungus in lukewarm water until softened. When reconstituted, the fungus can expand up to four times its dried size. Remove the hard stem, wash and drain. Slice fungus to required size.

- **Dried shiitake mushroom**
  Pset kra ob

Dried shiitake mushroom (*Lentinus edodes*) offers a rich nutty flavour and firm texture. It is sold fresh or dried. Before using, the dried form should be reconstituted by soaking in lukewarm water.

- **Straw mushroom**
  Pset chhambeung

This brown mushroom (*Volvariella volvacea*) is also known as paddy straw mushroom. The name refers to the beds of paddy straws on which the mushrooms are cultivated. They can also be found growing wild. The mushrooms have a delicate sweet and nutty flavour. Fresh straw mushrooms are uncommon outside Asia, so replace with oyster mushrooms. Canned straw mushroom is not a satisfactory substitute as its texture and flavour have been lost.

N

Neem, young leaves and flowers
Sdav

Young leaves and flowers of the neem tree (*Azadirachta indica*) are mostly available in January. They are enjoyed as a bitter vegetable and served specifically as an accompaniment to grilled fish.

The young leaves and flowers are blanched for a few minutes to reduce their bitterness.

Noodles, fresh and dried
There are many varieties of noodles made from different flours milled from rice, wheat or mung bean. In addition, noodles exist in an abundance of shapes, sizes and thickness and they are available fresh or dried.

- **Fresh rice noodles, other**

There are many different types of fresh rice noodles and they are used specifically for different dishes. For example, to make noodle soup (*kuteav*), thin flat rice noodles are called for, while vegetable stir-fries would call for large, flat or round rice noodles.

- **Fresh rice vermicelli** ***Nom ban chok***

Rice vermicelli is made from rice flour. In Cambodia, the white, thin and round strands are made daily and sold freshly cooked in markets. They are rolled up into nest-like bundles and displayed in bamboo baskets, lined with banana leaves.

Fresh rice vermicelli feature in various dishes and in curries. They are served cold, as an accompaniment.

Substitute: Dried rice vermicelli or Japanese *somen* noodles

- **Fresh udon noodles**

Udon are thick Japanese noodles made by kneading wheat flour with water and salt. *Udon* noodles are an acceptable substitute for round, fresh rice noodles.

- **Dried mung bean, vermicelli (Glass noodles)**

Mung bean vermicelli is made from mung bean starch. Before using, they should be soaked in lukewarm water until softened. Once cooked, the strands become translucent which is why they are sometimes referred as glass noodles or cellophane noodles.

Mung bean vermicelli is added to soups, meat stuffings and spring roll fillings, salads and stir-fries.

- **Dried rice vermicelli**

Dried rice vermicelli, also known as rice sticks, are thin white noodles made from rice flour. The long strands are folded into blocks and sold in packages.

They are a good substitute for fresh rice vermicelli but they should be prepared beforehand. Bring a pot of water to the boil, add dried rice vermicelli and cook until softened. Drain and rinse under cold running water before using.

Dried rice vermicelli can also be deep-fried. In this case, no soaking is required beforehand. Serve in *mi bam pong* (crispy rice vermicelli with garnish, page 160).

- **Dried somen noodles**

Like *udon*, *somen* are white Japanese noodles made of wheat flour. However, *somen* are very thin and can be served cold. They are a good substitute for fresh rice vermicelli (*nom ban chok*).

To cook *somen*, bring water to the boil and add noodles. Salt or oil is not needed. Cook for 2 minutes or until noodles are firm yet tender. Rinse with cold water and drain.

O

Oyster sauce ***Teuk kyan***
Originally, oyster sauce was made by cooking oysters over low heat for a long time until a thick, dark brown sauce was yielded. Today, most oyster sauces are flavoured with extract of oysters. Before buying, read carefully the label and choose a premium brand, selecting a product with less monosodium glutamate (MSG), if you can. The condiment is available in glass bottles from Asian stores and well-stocked supermarkets.

Oyster sauce, with its savoury flavour and a hint of sweetness, is commonly used to season stir-fries. Once opened, keep refrigerated.

P

Palmyra palm tree ***Tnaot***
Palmyra palm trees (*Borassus flabellifer*), also known as sugar palm trees, are a national emblem of Cambodia. The picturesque sight of Palmyra palm trees, standing majestically against a backdrop of mountains and under a clear blue sky, is a typical image of Cambodia.

Many Cambodians have sugar palm trees on their land, as they are a very important resource. All parts of the tree are used.

The hard and durable timber is prized for construction, the leaves are used to cover roofs and are woven into various handcrafted objects such as baskets, mats and hats. Young, green fruit is used in soups and desserts while ripe fruit is eaten fresh or candied. The sap can be consumed straightaway as a drink or processed into palm sugar, palm vinegar or palm wine.

- **Palm fruit** ***Plè tnaot***

Palm fruit is round, about the size

of a coconut, with a hard, green shell. Once the top is removed, three translucent, jelly-like seeds are revealed. The seeds are the edible part of the fruit.

As the fruit matures, the shell turns purple, then orange-yellow when ripe. Inside, the seeds become harder and the surrounding pulp, more fibrous. As such, the seeds are best consumed, fresh or cooked, when the fruit is young. Fresh, the fruit itself has little taste but served with crushed ice, it is a refreshing dessert, enjoyed on hot sunny days. Sliced thinly, the young seeds are specifically added to *samlar kâko tnaot* soup.

Harder, ripe seeds are candied (*tnaot chhoeung skar*) while the liquid extracted from the fibrous pulp is used in a dessert (*nom tnaot*).

- **Palm sugar** ***Skar tnaot***

Palm sugar comes from the sap

of the sugar palm tree. Collecting the sap requires physical strength so this is more a man's job. Late in the afternoon, the villagers climb the long bamboo poles laid against the trees. When they reach the top, they make a cut in the stems on which the fruit and flowers grow. The stems are inserted into bamboo tubes and safely tied up. The villagers leave the containers overnight to collect the sap. The next day, at dawn, the villagers come back to gather the bamboo tubes full of sap.

The sap can be consumed fresh but villagers typically choose to make palm sugar to earn extra income after the rice harvest is over.

Traditionally, the sap is cooked slowly over low heat and in large pans, with women stirring constantly, until thick and golden brown. Palm sugar is then poured into little palm-leaf cups to solidify.

Palm sugar imparts its distinctive aroma, colour and sweet taste to many dishes. It is used extensively in Khmer cuisine, mainly in desserts. In savoury dishes, palm sugar is used to balance the saltiness of the other ingredients and to caramelise pork or fish.

Palm sugar is available in liquid, solid or granular forms. Solid palm sugar is sold in coarse brown cakes or in blocks, contained in plastic tubs. Solid palm sugar can be quite hard; pound in a mortar the quantity required, until reduced to powder.

Palm sugar is now more readily available in supermarkets and natural food stores, as health conscious consumers become aware of its properties (low glycemic index).

Substitute: Brown sugar

Papaya, green ***L'hong***

The skin of the young, oval fruit

(*Carica papaya*) is green. Inside, there is a central cavity filled with numerous shiny round, black seeds surrounded by pale flesh. The flesh has little taste but it is crunchy and firm. As such, the young fruit (or green papaya) is very popular in dips, pickles or shredded in salads. It can also be cooked in soups, such as *samlar kâko*.

Young green papaya is a good meat tenderiser due to an enzyme called papain, contained in the fruit.

When the fruit ripens, the skin turns yellow-orange and the flesh, yellow-orange or yellow-red, depending on the variety of papaya. The flesh becomes sweeter and the texture softer, like ripe mangoes. Ripe papaya is used in desserts.

Pepper *M'rec*

Pepper (*Peper nigrum*) comes from the pepper vine. Growing in clusters, the small round, green berries become dark red when fully mature.

Kampot, a southwestern province of Cambodia, is renowned for producing one of the world's best pepper. Before the 1970s, French gourmet chefs had a constant supply of the fragrant spice shipped over to France. The finest restaurants in Paris could not be seen without it. But the Khmer Rouge regime of 1975 to 1979 changed all that. The pepper plantations were abandoned and destroyed, then replaced with rice cultivation. However, the plantations are now slowly recovering and this rare, highly sought-after pepper is produced again, in very small quantities.

Kampot pepper has a warm aroma, with a hint of eucalyptus.

- **Peppercorns, black**

Black peppercorns are whole berries picked when they reach maturity and turn red in colour. The stems are discarded, the berries sorted, then sun-dried until wrinkled and black. Black peppercorns can be crushed or ground and are described as black pepper. The aroma is earthy and the taste pungent.

- **Peppercorns, green**

Green peppercorns are the berries

picked from the vine while they are immature. The green berries are harvested, still on their long stems. They are consumed fresh. They are available in Asian supermarkets.

Substitute: Green peppercorns pickled in brine or vinegar but the taste is not comparable.

- **Peppercorns, white**

White pepper are whole berries picked ripe. The stems are discarded, berries sorted and their dark red skins removed, revealing a white inside which is sun-dried. Milder than black peppercorns, with a delicate flavour, white peppercorns are widely used as seasoning in Khmer cuisine. It can also be used in light-coloured dishes and sauces where black pepper would spoil the appearance.

Prahok *see* Fish, fermented

Prawn (shrimp), dried
Bangkear kriem

These are small little prawns, boiled in salted water, then sun-dried. Before using, soak in lukewarm water to soften and reduce saltiness. Drain and coarsely pound. Sprinkled on salads, dried prawn add colour, texture and an intense flavour. Use sparingly as it is salty.

Prawn (shrimp), giant freshwater
Bangkang teuk sab

Giant freshwater prawns are found in fresh waters across Southeast Asia. They are blue-tinged when raw. Once cooked, the prawns have a plump, lobster-like texture with a mild and sweet taste. They are done when they just turn pink.

Substitute: Saltwater king prawns (jumbo shrimps)

Prawn (shrimp), paste *Kapik*

This condiment is made from very small prawns that have been salted, fermented and sun-dried. The mixture is then pounded into a smooth paste.

Pinkish-grey or dark brown in colour, with a strong smell, it can be used raw as a dipping sauce for green mangoes, ambarella and green tamarind. Enjoying this paste is an acquired taste.

It is added to *kroeungs* and curries. To enhance the aroma, wrap the paste in banana leaves and dry-roast before using.

Prawn paste is available in Asian stores.

R

Rice

- **Rice, flour**

Rice flour comes from finely milled rice. It is used mainly in desserts. It is sold in Asian supermarkets.

- **Rice, sticky (glutinous) rice**

Sticky rice, also known as glutinous rice, requires a long soak in water before steaming. When cooked, the rice will approximately double in volume. It becomes sticky and translucent. Sticky rice is used for desserts and savoury dishes.

There are two varieties of sticky rice, the white and the black. Black sticky rice is in reality dark purple. It has a richer and nuttier flavour than white sticky rice and is mainly used for desserts. White and black sticky rice are available from Asian stores.

- **Rice, sticky (glutinous) rice flour**

Sticky rice flour is made from finely milled sticky rice. It is mostly used in desserts.

Rice paddy herb *M'aam*

This green herb (*Limnophila*

aromatica) grows in clumps, with narrow stems and small pointed leaves. In Cambodia, there are two varieties, one growing wild in flooded rice fields and water-submersed lands (*m'aam srè*) and one cultivated in gardens (*m'aam dey*). *M'aam srè* has longer stems and is more fragrant than *m'aam dey*. However, it is less commonly found in markets, outside the wet season.

Rice paddy herb is mostly used in sour soups for its sharp lemony flavour.

Rice paper (spring roll) wrappers

Rice paper wrappers are made

from a mixture of rice flour and water, dried on bamboo mats, giving the paper that characteristic crisscross pattern. Thin and almost translucent and brittle, they come in different shapes (round or square) and sizes. Handle with care to avoid breaking them.

Rice paper wrappers are used to wrap food. Before use, they need to be dipped briefly in a shallow dish of warm water, to soften and to become pliable. Do not allow to soak as paper rice will soften too much and tear easily.

Once soft, they can be eaten uncooked (in summer rolls) or cooked (in fried spring rolls). When fried, rice paper becomes crisp. For even lighter and crisper rolls, try brick pastry sheets (*feuilles de brick*) instead of rice paper wrappers.

Rice paper wrappers are available in many supermarkets and Asian stores. They come as individual sheets, tightly wrapped in a package. They can be kept almost indefinitely when stored in a dry place. When removed from the package and in contact with moisture, sheets tend to curl up. Keep them wrapped and remove from the pack just before using.

S

Shallots *Ktim kraham*

Shallots are predominant in Khmer

cuisine. The taste of Khmer shallots is similar to the Western variety but they are smaller and their skins are pinkish-purple in colour. They are available from Asian supermarkets.

Soy Products

- **Bean curd (Tofu)** ***Tavhou***

Bean curd, also known as soy bean curd or tofu, is made by curdling soy milk with a coagulant. A soft white product, bean curd has a neutral taste and little flavour of its own, allowing it to absorb flavours easily.

Bean curd is available in various forms. Firm bean curd is dense and can be cubed, stir-fried, smoked, marinated or served in soups. Silken bean curd is soft and creamy in texture and best for blended dishes.

Fresh bean curd is sold in water-filled packs and cartons, in supermarkets, natural food shops and Asian supermarkets. Keep in water unused quantities and store in the refrigerator. It should last several days, provided the water is changed daily.

- **Salted soy beans** ***Sieng***

This condiment is made of soy beans that are steamed, fermented with salt and wheat for about 2 weeks, then bottled. In appearance, the brown beans resemble coffee beans and have a characteristic salty flavour. Salted soy beans are used whole or chopped to season steamed and fried fish and noodle dishes.

- **Soy sauce, light and dark** ***Teuk si'iv***

Soy sauce is made by fermenting soy beans. There are two varieties of soy sauce, light and dark. Light soy sauce is saltier, with a more delicate flavour. It is the main soy sauce used for seasoning. Dark soy sauce is a darker, thicker sauce, with a slightly sweeter flavour than light soy sauce. In these recipes, dark soy sauce is mostly used in caramelised dishes.

Star anise ***Pkar chhan***

Star anise (*Illicium verum*) is the

fruit of a small tree native to southern China. The name refers to the shape of the fruit, resembling an eight-pointed star. Each point, or pod, contains a shiny, brown seed. Star anise has a liquorice-like flavour.

The spice can be added whole to the cooking pot and removed when the dish is served, or they can be left for decorative purposes. Star anise can also be used ground in preparations such as *saramann kroeung* and five-spice powder.

Starfruit ***Spue***

Starfruit or carambola (*Averrhoa*

carambola)), is a fruit of a tree native to Indonesia. The name refers to the shape of the fruit, resembling a five-pointed star when cut crosswise. The fruit is light green and as it matures, becomes yellow-orange. The entire fruit is edible, both the juicy flesh and the slightly waxy skin.

In Cambodia, starfruit is mostly eaten young, when it is sour, served sliced in a platter of mixed vegetables. Starfruit discolours easily when sliced. Drizzle with lemon juice, as you cut it.

T

Tamarind, fresh pods and pulp ***Ampil***

Tamarind (*Tamarindus indica*) is

a light brown pod that grows on tamarind trees. The pod contains large shiny seeds covered with a dark brown pulp, which can be very sweet to very sour, depending on the variety of tamarind. The sweet variety is eaten fresh or candied. The sour variety is widely used in Khmer cuisine as a souring agent in soups, salads and sauces. It is the juice extracted from tamarind that gives sourness to dishes.

Tamarind, juice

In these recipes, always use sour tamarind to extract the juice. The traditional way is to use fresh pods or pulp (techniques to extract juice, page 35). This takes time, so for convenience, opt for tamarind concentrate or powder. Fresh tamarind pods, pulp, concentrate and powder are available in Asian and Indian markets.

Substitute: Lime juice

Tamarind, young leaves ***Sleuk ampil***

Used as a vegetable, the young leaves of the tamarind tree impart a sour flavour to soups. The taste is reminiscent of sorrel, which can be used as substitute.

Tapioca pearls, small

Tapioca pearls are made of tapioca

flour, a starch extracted from the root of the cassava plant (also called manioc). The name refers to the pearl-like shape and colour of the ingredient. Tapioca pearls are commonly used as a thickener in dishes and are available in various sizes. For desserts, choose the small white pearls and use sparingly to give a smooth and sticky texture.

The pearls must be rinsed, soaked in warm water and drained before being cooked. Opaque when uncooked, the pearls become soft, swollen and completely translucent when well cooked. There should be no white dots in the middle.

T'chi *see* Aromatic herbs, fresh

Trey *see* Fish

Turmeric ***Romiet***

Turmeric (*Curcuma longa*) belongs

to the ginger family. The fresh root has a brown-beige skin. Once peeled off, a vibrant yellow-orange flesh is revealed. Unlike the other members of the ginger family, turmeric tastes rather mild, with no sharp bite. It has a peppery aroma, with a warm and slightly bitter flavour. Turmeric lends its distinctive colour and delicate flavour to many dishes. It is an essential ingredient in *kroeungs*.

Turmeric leaves are also used to perfume soups.

Use turmeric sparingly as only little is needed to impart its flavour and colour. The root should be peeled and chopped before being pounded. When handling fresh turmeric, wear rubber gloves as the deep colour stains fingers, clothes and utensils.

Traditionally, turmeric has been used as a natural dye, colouring the saffron robes of Buddhist monks. In addition, turmeric has been renowned for its medicinal properties, as a powerful anti-inflammatory agent to treat a variety of conditions. In the countryside, women, after childbirth or during their periods, rub on their body ground turmeric to treat skin problems.

Fresh turmeric is sold in Asian supermarkets.

Substitute: Powdered turmeric ($^{1}/_{2}$ tsp powder replaces 1-cm ($^{1}/_{2}$-in) knob fresh turmeric)

W

Water lily, young stems ***Pralit***

Water lily (*Nymphaeaceae*) is an

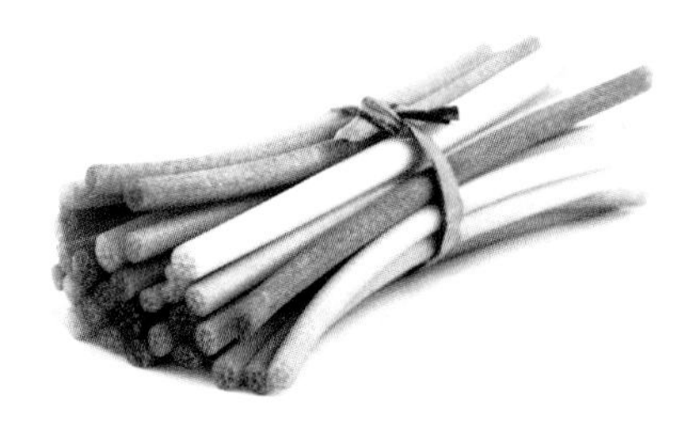

aquatic plant, sometimes mistaken for lotus. Water lilies have fragrant flowers of various colours and large shield-shaped leaves, which float on the water surface. Lotus flowers come in shades of pink or white and both flowers and leaves stand high above the water line.

Young stems of water lilies are consumed fresh or added to soups.

Water lily stems have a tough skin that should be peeled off before using (see technique, page 206).

Water spinach ***Trakuon***

Also called water convolvulus or

water morning glory, this plant (*Ipomoea aquatica*) grows easily in emerged water, thriving in fresh ponds and marshes. Both the stems and the arrow-shaped leaves are edible but the tender shoots and younger leaves are preferred to the tougher and more hollow stems.

Valued for its mild taste and crunchy texture, water spinach is very popular in Khmer cuisine. It is rich in iron and is inexpensive. Water spinach is consumed fresh, in salads or as an accompaniment, served on a platter with a selection of vegetables. They are tasty in soups and stir-fries.

White cabbage ***Spei kdaub***

White cabbage (*Brassica oleracea var. capitata)* is a round, compact and heavy vegetable, with tightly wrapped leaves. The outer pale green leaves get whiter towards the centre. This variety of cabbage is preferred because of its crunchy texture, and when cooked, the sturdy, smooth leaves don't get mushy. White cabbage can be pickled, consumed raw in salads or cooked in soups and stir-fries.

White radish

Also known as daikon (*Raphanus sativus*), this vegetable is a long, heavy radish, with a white skin. Inside, the white flesh is crisp and juicy, with a sweet peppery flavour. Choose radishes that are firm and unwrinkled. Use in soups, salads and to make pickles.

White radish is available in Asian stores and in well-stocked supermarkets.

Winged beans ***Popeay chhrung***

The winged bean plant

(*Psophocarpus tetragonolobus*) grows as a vine, with climbing stems and leaves. It is also known as four-angled bean, a name derived from its appearance. The bright green pods have four frilly edges running the length of each pod. A cross section of the bean shows a rectangle-like shape. All parts of the winged bean, the purple flower and young shoots are edible. Valued for its highly nutritious content and crunchy texture, winged bean is very much enjoyed fresh as an accompaniment, served with a selection of vegetables. It can also be added to stir-fries and soups, specifically *samlar kâko* soup.

Wood apple ***Krassaing***

Wood apple (*Feronia limonia*) is the

fruit of a tree native to India and grown throughout Southeast Asia. In Cambodia, there are two varieties of wood apple. The common variety (*krassaing si plê*) has a white centre and is edible whereas the other rarer variety (*krassaing pul*), with a purplish centre, is poisonous.

Krassaing si plê, is a sour fruit about the size of a small orange. It has a hard green shell which has to be cracked using a heavy cleaver. Inside are yellow-brown seeds, surrounded by white sticky pulp. The pulp and seeds are used as a souring agent in various Khmer dishes, such as sour soups.

Depending on the recipe, replace wood apple with tamarind juice or lime juice.

The Secrets of Success

WEIGHTS AND MEASURES

These recipes are family recipes which have been handed down orally from mother to daughter for many generations. As can be expected, measuring cups, kitchen scales and timers were not used in traditional Cambodian cooking, so quantities, preparation and cooking times were rarely specified.

However, when passing down these recipes to my daughter, Kanika, I realised that she was unfamiliar with cooking and new to Khmer dishes, so it would be difficult for her to gauge the quantities and arrive at a specific taste or flavour for these dishes. She needed guidance, so I tested the recipes one by one and wrote down the measures for the ingredients and the cooking times.

The measures are the result of my own experiments, which I have provided as much as possible by teaspoons (5 g / 1/6 oz), tablespoons (15 g / 1/2 oz) and handfuls. When it comes to seasoning the dishes and using *prahok* however, the quantities may look rather vague, but this is to give the cook plenty of scope to modify the quantities according to personal taste. Feel free to experiment, follow your instinct and play around with flavours and aromas. Remember that you can always adjust the seasoning just before serving.

Serving quantities mentioned in this book are indicative only. In Cambodia, dishes are rarely served in individual portions but rather, everyone helps themselves from large platters placed on the dining table. The dishes can also be mixed and matched for serving together and do not follow any particular order.

COOKING TERMS

Bain-marie

This is a method of slow cooking where the food item is placed in a container which is in turn placed over a large pot of boiling water.

Blanch

To immerse briefly in boiling water.

Brown

To make or to become brown through heating.

Bruise

To crush or pound. For example, lemongrass stalks are flattened using the blade of a large knife or a pestle, until the fibres are crushed to release its fragrance.

Butterfly

To split (a piece of meat) almost in two and spread it out flat so it cooks more evenly. Chicken or prawns (shrimps) are typically butterflied.

Chiffonade

To shred or finely cut leaf vegetables (lettuce, cabbage or herbs). An easy way to do this is to roll a leaf up, then slice it crosswise.

Dry-roast

To roast over low to medium heat without fat or oil, stirring constantly, until golden brown and the aroma of the ingredients is released.

Julienne

To cut into long and thin matchstick-size strips.

Marinate

To place food, usually meat or seafood, and occasionally vegetables, in seasoning or aromatic ingredients to flavour the food.

Mince

To chop food into very small or fairly small pieces using a knife or mincer.

Pare (a fruit)

To remove skin, white pith, pips, seeds and stones from a fruit and only keep the flesh (for example, a grapefruit).

Season

To add condiments (salt, pepper, spices, aromatic herbs) to bring out the flavour of a dish.

Shred

To cut food into narrow strips, using a knife, grater or food processor fitted with a shredding disk.

Simmer

To heat at a temperature below the boiling point so that food cooks slowly.

Skim

To remove the foam that forms on the surface of a liquid, usually stock or broth, during cooking.

Snip

To cut with scissors in small quick strokes rather than chopping with a knife.

Stir-fry

To cook briefly in a wok or pan over high heat, while stirring briskly.

PREPARING INGREDIENTS FOR SALADS

Meat and seafood

If raw or marinated in lemon juice, the salad is called a *p'lear*, if cooked, it is known as a *gnoam*.

Vegetables

Vegetables should be peeled if necessary, then washed and finely sliced. Soak vegetables in ice cold water to give them a good crunch. Drain well before using.

Smoked fish

Grill in an oven or dry-roast in a wok to revive flavour and texture and to remove easily skin and bones.

Dried prawns (shrimps)

Rinse, then soak in lukewarm water for 10 minutes. Drain and pound coarsely.

Fresh aromatic herbs

Choose an assorted bunch of fresh herbs as desired. Rinse and drain or pat-dry. Add to dishes just before serving to avoid them wilting.

Dry-roasted peanuts

Unsalted peanuts are preferred. If using salted peanuts, reduce the amount of salt or fish sauce in the recipe. Crush the peanuts coarsely to just get some bite from the nuts.

Fried garlic and shallots

Peel and slice thinly before frying (page 34).

Chillies

The use and addition of chillies is optional. Serve in individual saucers on the side for guests to help themselves to according to taste. Alternatively, chop or crush and add to the salad dressing.

Salad dressing

Drizzle dressing over salad and serve the remainder separately so that each guest can add more dressing according to taste. Ideally, the dressing should not be prepared in advance as this will affect its taste. If prepared beforehand, taste and adjust seasoning just before using. Cambodian dressings are typically salty, sweet and sour in taste.

P'lear

P'lear refers to salads where the meat, fish or seafood are cold-cooked by marinating in lemon juice.

1. Select raw beef, fish or seafood
2. Marinate in lemon juice
3. Prepare dressing with juice extracted from the marinade
4. Combine and toss marinated beef, fish or seafood with dressing and vegetables
5. Garnish with fresh aromatic herbs, unsalted dry-roasted peanuts, fried garlic and shallots and chillies (optional)

Gnoam

Gnoam refers to salads where the ingredients are cooked.

1. Select cooked meat or seafood
2. Combine and toss meat or seafood with dressing
3. Add vegetables
4. Stir in smoked fish and dried prawns

PREPARING INGREDIENTS

Spring rolls

Summer rolls

Water lily or young lotus stems

Water lily (see photos below) and young lotus stems have a tough and stringy layer that should be peeled and discarded. Cut the stems into 4-cm (1½-in) sections.

Leave to soak in a bowl of cold water to prevent discolouration and make pulling off the remaining fibres easier.

Dip a pair of wooden chopsticks in the bowl and rub them between your palms to catch any remaining fibres.

Prawns (shrimps)

Buying and storing prawns

Prawns can be bought fresh or frozen, raw or cooked, shelled or unshelled. For these recipes, fresh raw prawns, with the shell on, are preferred. When choosing prawns, select those with firm flesh, intact shells and no smell.

Store prawns in their original packaging in the refrigerator and use within a day. Alternatively place in the freezer to keep for several weeks.

Frozen prawns should be rinsed under cold running water, drained and placed in a covered container in the refrigerator to thaw.

Preparing prawns

To remove the shell, grip the body of the prawn in one hand and twist the head off with the other. Pull off the legs and remove the shell.

Some recipes call for the head and the tail, or just the tail, to be left intact.

The greenish black "vein" running along the back of the prawn is the intestinal tract. Using a small pointed knife, make a shallow cut along the back of the prawn and pull out the tract. Rinse prawns and drain well.

Both raw and cooked prawns are deveined the same way.

Crabs

For these recipes, fresh whole crabs are preferred. Choose crabs that are lively and smell of fresh seawater. Live crabs can be stored for 1 or 2 days in the refrigerator.

To put the crab to sleep and to firm the flesh, soak them in ice cold water for 30 minutes. Scrub the shell well and rinse.

Holding the crab firmly in place, insert the tip of a knife under the carapace and lift it off. Remove and discard the grey gills. Twist and pull off the tips of the legs. Using a heavy cleaver, crack the claws. Cut them into two or four parts according to the size of the crabs.

Squid and cuttlefish

Squid

Pull off squid head and tentacles from the body (see photos below). The gut should also come away at the same time. Pull out the transparent quill from inside the tube. Cut off the fins at the side of the tube. Discard the gut, quill and fins. Cut off the section of the head where the eyes are and discard. Rinse the squid head.

Pull off the thin purple skin from the squid tube. Rinse squid tube in cold water. With a sharp knife, score squid tube with crisscross cuts.

Cuttlefish

Cut the body cavity on the soft side, open out, remove and discard cuttlebone and gut. Cut off tentacles from head, just below the eyes. Remove the cuttlebone and discard the head. Pull off the skin and rinse well. Cut the body into squares or strips. If cutting squares, score with crisscross cuts.

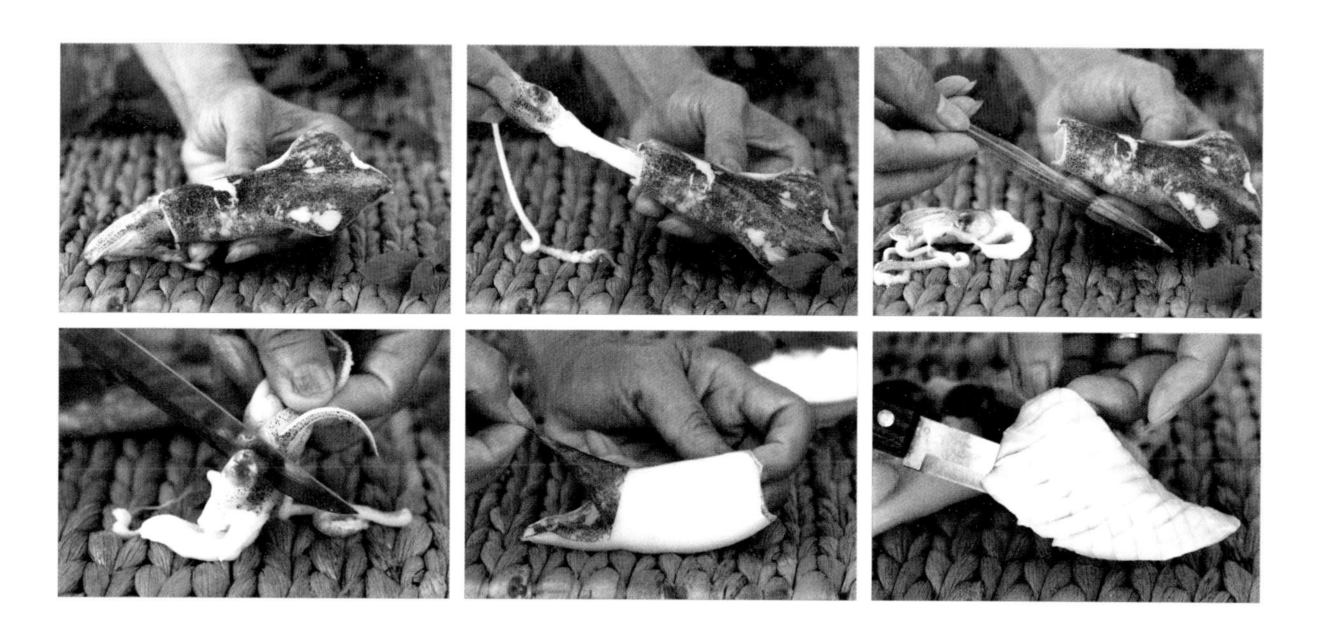

CUTTING TECHNIQUES

In Cambodian cuisine, ingredients are usually cut into pieces before being cooked.

Vegetables

Vegetables are diced, sliced, julienned or cut into strips or slivers.

Meat and fish

Meat is cut into chunks for curries or sliced thinly for stir-fries. This ensures that the pieces remain tender and that the cooking times for both meat and vegetables are similar. Beef should be cut across the grain, but pork and poultry should be cut along the grain.

Fish is filleted, cut into steaks or used whole for a variety of dishes including soups, salads and stir-fries.

Cutting cucumbers for salad

Cut each cucumber into 5-cm (2-in) sections (see photos below). Using a paring knife, peel the cucumber skin in a continuous strip. Roll up the skin and slice it crosswise into fine strips. Set aside.

Use the same peeling and slicing technique for cucumber flesh. Discard the soft centre and seeds.

Cutting pineapple

Cut off the leafy top and bottom of the pineapple. Cut off skin using a sharp knife.

To remove the eyes, cut at an angle behind each one, following the lines they form.

Halve the pineapple lengthwise, then cut into four sections. Remove the hard core.

Cut into slices for stir-fries and desserts, into small strips for soups or into cubes for fruit salads.

COOKING TECHNIQUES

Steaming

This method of cooking ensures that the ingredients remain tender and retain their taste, texture and nutritional value (vitamins and minerals). Bamboo steamers are ideal for steaming but stainless steel and electric steamers work just as well.

Bamboo steamer

A traditional bamboo steamer is an authentic way to steam food. Bamboo steamers come in various sizes. Choose a wide one, around 30 cm (12 in), so it will be large enough to steam a whole fish or enough rice for a family meal.

The bamboo steamer and lid are placed directly over a wok filled with water. As the water in the wok is heated, the steam rises under and around the food, cooking it gently. Always keep the lid on the steamer and ensure that there is enough water in the wok.

A stainless steel steamer can be a substitute for a bamboo one. However, it will not impart the distinct and subtle flavours that a bamboo steamer will.

Bamboo steamers are available in Asian markets and major department stores.

Cooking with a wok, sauté pan or frying pan

The wok is central to Cambodian cooking. Made of steel, it is a versatile utensil with many uses, from deep-frying, boiling, roasting, braising, stir-frying to steaming. A wok heats up very fast, with uniform heat distribution. Round bottomed woks work well on gas rings. Alternatively, use a sauté or frying pan on electric hobs.

For stir-frying, heat oil in a wok over medium heat. Add the ingredients as instructed in the recipe and stir-fry briefly over high heat, stirring and tossing frequently. This quick cooking method ensures that ingredients retain their flavour and texture: meat remains tender and vegetables crunchy.

Cook small portions in succession rather than all at once to obtain the best flavour.

Barbecuing using a wood fire

Make sure that the charcoal is smouldering before grilling food. Keep a bottle of water at hand and sprinkle over the charcoal occasionally to keep it from bursting into flames.

For meat, choose only pieces that are best suited for barbecuing. When cooking meat that has been stored in the refrigerator, remember to bring it to room temperature beforehand.

Season or marinate meat before grilling it. To avoid charring, never barbecue food on top of flaming charcoal. Use only glowing embers.

Charcoal grilling helps to remove some of the fat in meat. For an even grill, use tongs to turn meat over from time to time while cooking. Barbecue forks tend to puncture the meat and cause the juices to flow out, resulting in meat that is dry.

Use tongs to check if the meat is cooked to your liking by squeezing the meat. Rare feels soft, medium rare has little resistance while well done feels quite firm.

Always add fresh aromatic herbs when cooking is over, so that they remain fragrant. However, dried herbs should be added a few minutes before the end of grilling to allow time for their aroma to develop.

For safety reasons, never use alcohol or flammable liquids to light the fire. Use small twigs or barbecue lighters instead. If using wooden skewers, soak in cold water for at least an hour beforehand to prevent them from catching fire and burning.

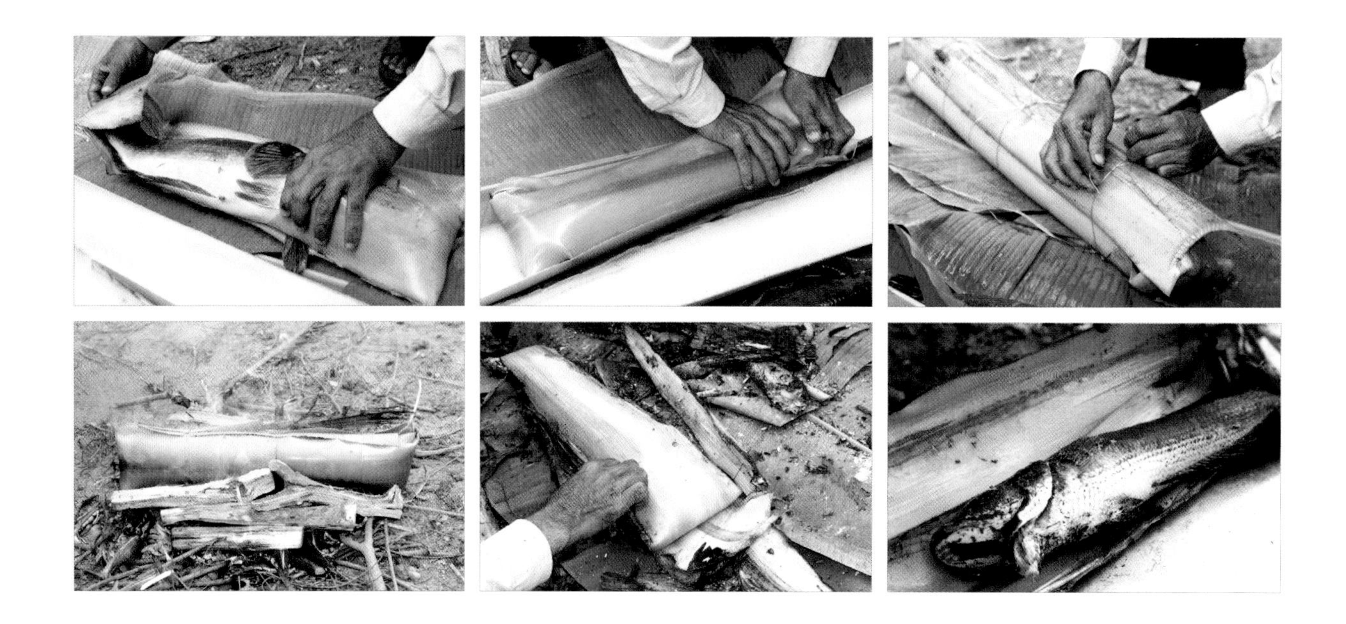

Fish grilled in banana trunk

In Cambodia, the banana tree's trunk is used as a wrap for grilling fish over fire or charcoal. It is a favourite activity for family outings to the countryside.

The outer layers of the banana tree's trunk is used. A fish is placed on a piece of banana trunk. The ends are folded over the fish to cover it, then secured with some wire.

The parcel is placed in the flames and left to cook. The precise cooking time is difficult to assess but it can range from 30 to 45 minutes, depending on the heat and the size of the fish. This cooking technique results in a very moist and flavourful fish with the banana trunk imparting its distinctive flavour to the fish.

The fish is usually served with fresh and crunchy vegetables, neem leaves and flowers as well as tamarind dipping sauce (page 45).

PERFUMING DESSERTS

Many Cambodian desserts are perfumed with flowers or smoked with beeswax.

Perfuming with flower-scented water

Fragrant jasmine flowers are the most popular choice, but other flowers such as roses can be used.

Ensure that flowers have not been treated with chemicals.

Steep flowers in water in a non-metallic bowl. Cover and leave overnight. Use quickly as the scent of the perfumed water is volatile.

Smoking with beeswax

Put a charcoal ember in a small dish. Place the dish in the middle of a large container, with the sweets to be smoked around it. Put a small piece of beeswax on the ember, then immediately cover the container with a lid. Leave for a few hours to allow the sweets to be wholly suffused.

Banana leaf cups

(for sticky rice balls filled with palm sugar, page 163)

Wipe banana leaves with a clean, moist tea towel. Soak for a few minutes in lukewarm water to soften and make leaves pliable for shaping.

Remove tough centre vein from banana leaves, then cut leaves into 10-cm (4-in) diameter circles. Make a 2-cm (3/4-in) fold on one side of the circle to create a cone and secure with toothpicks.

Make a base so the cone can sit on its own and becomes a cup. To do this, use your thumb to press down on the pointed tip of the cone, pushing it inward. Sit the cup on its base.

Banana leaf cups (for fish *amok*, page 74)

Wipe banana leaves with a clean, moist tea towel. Soak for a few minutes in lukewarm water to soften and make leaves pliable for shaping.

Remove tough centre vein from banana leaves. For small individual cups, cut leaves into 12-cm (5-in) diameter circles. For larger cups, cut leaves into 20–25-cm (8–10-in) diameter circles.

For each cup, stack two circles together. This will hold better the fish mixture.

Make a 1-cm (1/2-in) fold on the circle and secure with toothpicks. Repeat this step three times at regular intervals to create a cup.

Tomato carving

Blossoming rose

Select an average-size tomato that is bright red in colour, firm in texture and without any bruises. Wash and pat-dry the tomato.

Using a paring knife, cut off the stem end and peel the tomato skin in a continuous strip.

Roll the skin up, then flip it over and adjust to get the shape of a rose.

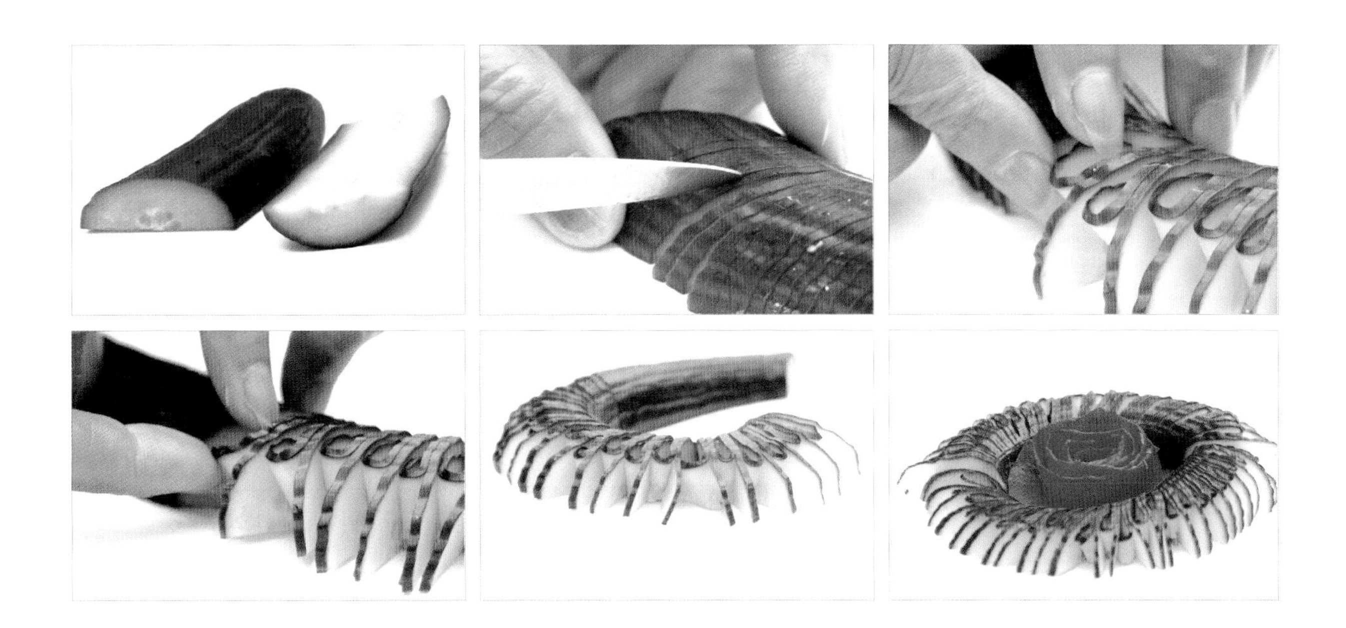

Cucumber carving

Cucumber flower

Select a long, straight cucumber. Trim ends, then halve the cucumber lengthwise.

Place one portion on a cutting board with the peel side up. Using a sharp, pointed knife, make diagonal thin cuts in cucumber, taking care that the slices remain attached at one end (about 0.5 cm / 1/4 in).

Fold over alternate slices, starting with the second slice and tucking the folded end in so it stays in place. Repeat steps for the remaining cucumber portion.

Form a circle with the shaped cucumber and place a carved tomato flower (page 218) in the middle.

Capsicum (bell pepper) carving

Capsicum flower

Select a medium-size capsicum in red, orange or yellow. It should have a firm and glossy skin and be without blemishes.

Using a marker pen, draw zigzag patterns around the circumference of the capsicum.

With the tip of a sharp, pointed knife, cut capsicum, following the lines. Separate the two halves of the capsicum. With the tip of the knife, slice every petal down in half, taking care that they remain attached at the base.

Using your hands, carefully pull the outer petals so they spread outwards. Make a V-shape cut on each outer petal.

Fold over each inner petal, tucking them in at the core.

Soak capsicum flower in ice cold water so petals become firm and spread nicely.

Onion carving

Onion flower

Choose a round, medium-size onion, free of blemishes.

Using a sharp, pointed knife, insert the tip of the blade into the onion, then make narrow zigzag cuts around the onion, making sure that you cut through to the centre of the onion.

Press the onion between your palms to help the onion separate more easily. Pull the two halves apart.

Soak the onion in ice cold water so that the petal designs become firm and spread nicely, like a blossoming flower.

Pour a little food colouring on petals. Remove from water and drain.

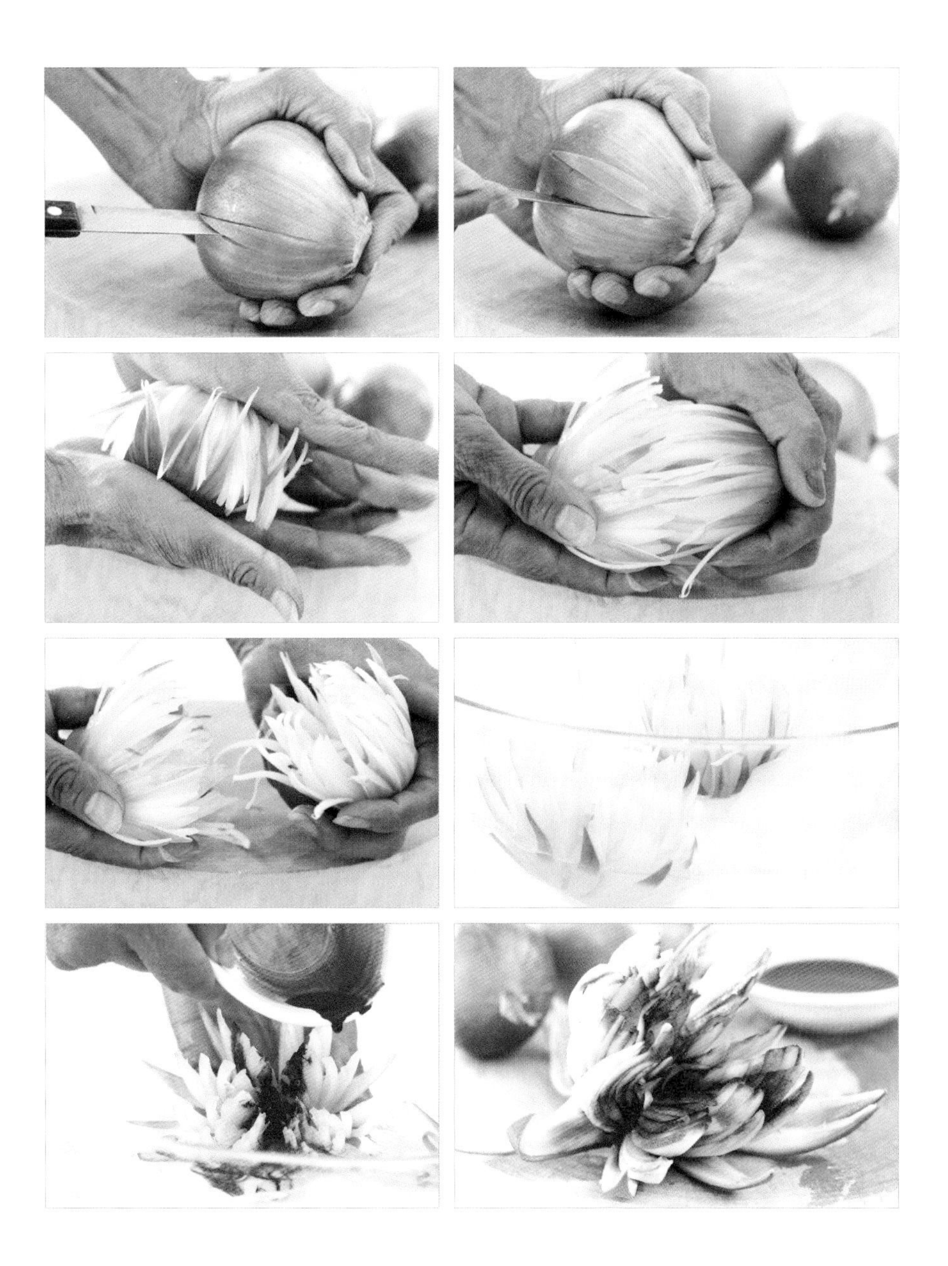

Index of Recipes

Cambodia on the World Map

Map of Cambodia & Its Provinces

Regional Delicacies

Battambang

- Rice
- *Samlar prahoeur tumpein*, a special kind of bamboo shoot soup
- Battambang *teuk kroeung* sauce (*bok m'preuk*)
- Smoked fish (*trey chhae*), made with *trey andeng*

Kampong Speu

- Palm sugar, palm wine

Kampot

- Fish and seafood, fish sauce, green peppercorns
- Durian
- Chicken with rice, Kampot-style
- Rice vermicelli, Kampot-style
- Bird's nest cakes (*nom sambok chhap*)
- Sticky rice cakes with grated coconut and palm sugar (*nom sleuk chak*)
  These cakes are wrapped in nipa palm (*chak*) leaves. The nipa palm tree (*nypa fruticans*) grows in abundance all over this province. These delicious treats can be bought from hawkers on Kompong Som beach.

Kandal

Taluon, my mother's birthplace

- Sugarcane, fruit and vegetables

Kompong Cham

- Grilled silkworms (*doek doeur*)
- Sticky rice cakes coated in sugar and shaped like a root of ginger (*nom k'gneï*)

Kompong Thom

- Smoked fish (*trey chhae*)
- Dried salted fish (*trey ngiet*)
- Fermented fish (*pha'ak*)

Kratie

Rocakandal, my birthplace

- Sticky rice grilled in bamboo sticks (*kralan*)
- Pomelos

Mondulkiri

- Rice wine, avocados
- Game

Prey Veng

- Ortolans (songbirds) in the town of Banam
- *A prèk ta sar*, a kind of cake similar to *kralan*
  It is made of rice flour, coconut milk and palm sugar and is steamed rather than grilled (*nom prâbos*).
- Deep-fried ortolans, served with a pepper and lime sauce

Pursat

- Oranges
- *Chek chvear* bananas, a variety containing many seeds

Rattanakiri

- Coffee, cashew nuts
- Honey
- Salad made of beef gut casing (*phear*)

Siem Reap

- *Prahok*, smoked fish (*trey chhae*), dried salted fish (*trey ngiet*)

Sihanoukville (Kompong Som)

- Fish and seafood

Stung Treng

- *Trey pase ee* (*Mekongina erythrospila*), a species of fish found in the Mekong River
- *Trey pava moukpi* (*Bangana behri*), another species of fish found in the Mekong River
- Salad made up of giblets, pork blood clots, shallots, lemongrass, bean sprouts and an assorted bunch of fresh aromatic herbs (*sék*)
- Fish and lemongrass salad (*lab*)

Takeo

Preah Ream, my father's birthplace

- Giant freshwater prawns (shrimps) from the Bati region
- Barbecued stuffed frogs (*kan kep baork*) at Ang Ta Som

Bibliography

Dictionnaire des plantes utilisées au Cambodge, Pauline Dy Phon

Fish base: http://www.fishbase.org

Ministry of Agriculture, Forestry and Fisheries (M.A.F.F), Cambodia

Inland Fisheries Research and Development Institute, Fisheries Administration
Poster Part I : Freshwater fishes in the Kingdom of Cambodia
Poster Part II : Freshwater catfish species in the Kingdom of Cambodia
Poster Part III : Freshwater fishes in the Kingdom of Cambodia

Acknowledgements

This book is dedicated to my beloved mother who, through food, taught me courage and strength of character in the face of adversity.

My older sister Sarabory Nhek helped me recall the flavours of our younger days. Her loving and serene presence has been a great support to me while I was working on the book.

To my son Sotta Long, I dedicate the steamed rice recipe. As a true Cambodian, he never eats a meal without rice! His enthusiasm, sense of humour and love helped me overcome many obstacles.

My heartfelt thanks go to Mr Phoeun Mak and Mr Phleng Loch for their contribution in transcribing words from the Khmer script into the Latin alphabet and reviewing the Cambodian traditions described in the book. Mr Phoeun Mak, formerly Research Director in Cambodian History at the National Centre of Scientific Research (Centre National de la Recherche Scientifique or CNRS) and Mr Phleng Loch, formerly professor of Khmer Language and Literature at the National Institute of Oriental Languages and Civilisations (Institut National des Langues et Civilisations Orientales or INALCO) have struck me by their intellectual rigour, vast knowledge, great patience and modesty.

I would also like to thank Mrs Ker Nol, my family and my friends for their valuable support, and last but not least, all the villagers in Cambodia who welcomed me with a smile and were always eager to share their traditional recipes.

Sorey Long

A little chocolate?

She knows everyone's personal culinary tastes inside out. She spoils everyone close to her by cooking their favourite delicacies. She can silently comfort and reassure any troubled soul, not with a handkerchief but with a tempting *babar* (rice congee) or a box of chocolate. Through her meals, she says "I love you". Thank you mother for this fabulous culinary adventure. It was a magical moment for me, a great way to spend more time with you and get to know you better through food.

A cup of linden herbal infusion?

My deep gratitude goes to Alexandre, my enthusiastic Tilleul. He gave me wings, trust and courage to undertake the project and to overcome hurdles. His contribution was vital. Without him, this book could not have been published. His quiet presence was soothing and calming, in times of rush, panic and short deadlines.

A juicy starfruit?

Many thanks to Sovann, who brought back, with the help of his grandfather, a beautiful starfruit from Siem Reap, for our photos. I spent many days and nights in front of the computer. As a result, I sometimes forgot to bring my children a snack after school or prepare their favourite meal. I am amazed by their level of understanding and forgiveness, for such young little people. I am forever indebted to Sovann, Séléna and Cyrus for their patience and love. I am filled with gratitude to have such fun and loving children. What a great honour to be their mother.

A birthday chocolate cake?

When I arrived in London and hardly knew anyone, Valérie welcomed me and celebrated my birthday with a homemade chocolate cake. She is a generous, witty and inspiring friend. From the very beginning, her unwavering support and insightful advice gave me the confidence to continue writing. Thank you for believing in the project, for your help in translating the Introduction and writing the Foreword.

Pass it on!

Finally, this book is dedicated to Sotta, my beloved brother, Botta, my father and friends, family and cousins, who have kindly offered support, time and skills to promote the book and our beautiful Cambodian culinary traditions.

Kanika Linden